"In the spirit of the Holy Family of Nazareth the Sisters strive to
live and work in simplicity, hospitality of heart, faith and charity.
They are witness to the good news and stand against conditions
that demean or undermine the dignity of persons or
the sacredness of the family."
Constitutions of Sisters of the Holy Family

A Legacy of Caring

THE IMPASSIONED MISSION OF SISTERS OF THE HOLY FAMILY

•

IN COMMEMORATION OF THEIR 125TH JUBILEE
NOVEMBER 6, 1997

WRITTEN, PHOTOGRAPHED AND DESIGNED BY
CHARLOTTE M. HALL AND JAMES WOLFE HALL

•

A Publication of Hall Media Group

A Legacy of Caring
The Impassioned Mission of Sisters of the Holy Family

Written by Charlotte M. Hall
Design and Contemporary Photography (except as noted) by Charlotte M. Hall & James Wolfe Hall
Historical Photographs from Archives of Sisters of the Holy Family
Graphics, Photo Restoration & Enhancement, and Pre-press by James Wolfe Hall

Published by Hall Media Group
1989A Santa Rita Road, Suite 300, Pleasanton, California 94566
Printed by Publishers Press, Salt Lake City, Utah

Library of Congress Catalog Card Number: 97-93185
International Standard Book Number 0-9657486-0-X

Additional copies may be ordered from:
Sisters of the Holy Family
PO Box 3248
Fremont California, 94539-0324
510-624-4596

Acknowledgements

First we must acknowledge and thank the Leadership Team
of Sisters of the Holy Family who believed in us and
entrusted this wonderful project to us.
Another thank you goes to everyone who graciously gave
of their time to be interviewed, especially each Sister
who allowed us into her life.

A special thanks to:
Neila Renfro for her diligent proofreading,
Sister Michaela O'Connor for the wealth of historical information she shared,
Rosemary Bevans-Lynch and Debbie Thomas for their unending friendship and support.

This book has consumed our lives for two years, and everyone who
knows us has put up with listening to us ramble about it.
To all of you - Thank you for your input, large and small.

Charlotte & Jim Hall

Thanks to These Individuals and Organizations Who Helped Underwrite This Book

Most Rev. John S. Cummins,
Diocese of Oakland, CA
Most Rev. Francis T. Hurley,
Archdiocese of Anchorage, AK
Most Rev. George H. Niederauer,
Diocese of Salt Lake City, UT
Most Rev. John T. Steinbock,
Diocese of Fresno, CA
Most Rev. Phillip F. Straling,
Diocese of Reno, NV
Most Rev. Daniel F. Walsh,
Diocese of Las Vegas, NV
Most Rev. Michael W. Warfel,
Diocese of Juneau, AK
Most Rev. William K. Weigand,
Diocese of Sacramento, CA

Ms. Catherine Barton
Ms. Ann Billeci
Ms. Paula M. Clark
Mr. and Mrs. Jack Knowles
Sister Loretta Marie Marbach,
in memory of Mr. and Mrs. Philip Marbach
Mr. and Mrs. Leon J. Mezzetti, Sr.
Mr. and Mrs. Fred J. Pedersen, Jr.
Mr. and Mrs. Raul Perez
Mr. and Mrs. Robert W. Spencer

Auxiliary of San Antonio Holy Family Guild
C.L.B.I. Investments, Inc.
Knights of Columbus Council #1489, Rapid City, SD
Long Beach Holy Family Guild
Mission San Jose Holy Family Guild
Peninsula Holy Family Guild
Southern Alameda County Theresians

Sister Elaine M. Sanchez, SHF

Congregational President, Sisters of the Holy Family

A Legacy of Caring

THE IMPASSIONED MISSION OF SISTERS OF THE HOLY FAMILY

Table of Contents

Foreword

A half century and more ago, I would awaken after my nap at the Holy Family Day Home at 16th and Dolores Streets in San Francisco. I would look up to the great windows through which streamed the California sunshine. The windows seemed vast and distant, as if they were the windows of a great cathedral. I later learned that the famous architect Willis Polk had designed the building; but even then, as a boy of five and six, I recognized that I was spending my days in distinguished surroundings, watched over by kindly women wearing the habit of the Sisters of the Holy Family. I remember the order and dignity of those days—and the serene stability that meant much to a child of divorced parents whose mother worked each day at a nearby bank in the Mission District. The Sisters of the Holy Family treated us with dignity and respect. I can never remember anything even vaguely approaching punishment, although all of us, boys and girls together, were well behaved. We quite naturally fell into the dignity of our surroundings, and the gracious care of the Sisters seemed to elicit our best behavior.

As a fourth generation San Franciscan, I was being cared for by a Community of Sisters whose origins and very spirit came from the City itself. Here, after all, was a Community founded in 1872—at the suggestion of Father John Joseph Prendergast and Archbishop Joseph Sadoc Alemany, OP—jointly by the privileged ward of a prominent local family, Elizabeth Armer, and her companion, Ellen O'Connor, a daughter of the Gold Rush who had come to California in a covered wagon at the age of three.

For eight years before these dedicated women made their formal novitiates, took their vows, and assumed their habits, they lived and worked together in San Francisco as a community of dedicated women en route to becoming a sisterhood. In a very real sense, San Francisco was providing them with their first novitiates; not the San Francisco of beauty, glamour and international reputation, but the San Francisco of young children of working parents who needed care and instruction, of shut-ins who required visits, of young and old alike needing catechetical instruction or the healing touch of a kind word.

The more we learn of early Christianity, the more we discover that in the first centuries of our religion, women, such as the first generations of Holy Family Sisters, also provided healing ministries in the great cities of the ancient world. Elizabeth Armer, Ellen O'Connor, and their growing group of companions were thus recapitulating and re-experiencing that ancient synergy between cities, charity and Christian women. In time, their association of women became a pontifically approved sisterhood. Elizabeth Armer became Sister M. Dolores, and Ellen O'Connor became Mother M. Teresa; but the simplicity of spirit, the flexibility, the emphasis upon charity and service that characterized those first formative years has remained with the Holy Family Sisters throughout their 125 year existence.

Because the Sisters of the Holy Family had concentrated upon the task at hand, and because they had always lived unpretentiously in a spirit of service, they were capable of bringing their mission with great success into the more diverse ministries of the post Vatican II environment. Their ministry began with day care, home visitation and catechetical instruction, mostly in the San Francisco Bay Area. Today, Sisters of the Holy Family administer parishes in Alaska, work with Mexican-American communities in Texas, train lay ministers in Hawaii, minister in family shelters in Nevada, care for the developmentally disabled and those afflicted with AIDS in California, give care to the terminally ill, including children, in a number of states, as well as carry on their traditional ministries of day care, home visitation, and catechesis throughout the Southwest, Far West, Alaska and Hawaii.

Perhaps more than ever do the Sisters of the Holy Family today resemble those tireless and generous women of the early Church. Even more powerfully—in their faith and courage, in their loyalty, and courageous commitment to their vocation—these great and good Sisters resemble an even earlier and more sacred band of women: those who stood steadfastly at the foot of the Cross and three days later were the first to share the glory of the Resurrection.

Dr. Kevin Starr
State Librarian of California
(Holy Family Day Home, 1945-1947)

Mission

*For one hundred twenty-five years,
the ministry of Sisters of the
Holy Family has been
a legacy of caring.
Most of this book is devoted
to telling you about their work,
but first you must know
who they are and
from where they came.*

A Blend of Constancy & Change

The soft fragrance of the jacaranda tree lingers in the air, squirrels scamper underneath it, and birds are filling its branches. I can never walk along this pathway without slowing my pace and marveling at the peace and beauty that pervades the grounds of the Motherhouse. Who would ever guess what treasure is at the end of the unassuming driveway off a busy street?

Tonight is installation of the new Leadership Team for Sisters of the Holy Family, the culmination of an election process held every four years. We are here to commemorate it with Mass and a dinner party. As always, Associate Carol Hernandez warmly greets me at the door. I am a little early, last minute details are still being done. I peek in the chapel. Someone is putting out the Communion bread; small, deep brown loaves homemade by Sister Isabel Anne Morey. Someone else is testing the microphone for the singers. Bright colorful banners hanging overhead add to the festive feel.

As people begin to arrive, I wave to some of the women I have not seen in months. They live all around the country, and many only come home once a year for this annual gathering. I watch them greet each other, obviously happy to be together. This year's gathering is a Chapter which is held every four years to elect leaders and make decisions about their common life and ministries. I reflect back on the past year I spent getting to know these women, Sisters of the Holy Family, and how totally misinformed I was about what it means to be a Sister.

I have seen a myriad of different places they work, from hospitals to churches, to county agencies. I have been with them at meetings and parties. I have been awed, inspired and educated by them. As an organization they are struggling with achieving the right balance between preserving their heritage and adapting to a changing world. As individuals they engage in the discussion, but are not deterred by it. They continue to do the work they feel compelled and called to do. There is more individualism within the group than I expected. The unity is their mission to families and children, and their charism...those unique qualities, beliefs and expressions that distinguish them, and which they all share.

The music starts and I am pulled back to the present. Like most everything else I have experienced with them, the service is a blend of constancy and change. The solemn procession bringing symbols of the past, carried by women dressed in contemporary clothes. The readings include both Biblical passages and an imaginative retelling of the story of creation which focuses on the role of men and women as partners with God. A priest presides, but most of the service is led by women.

At the end of the service, Congregational President Elaine Marie Sanchez greets each of us as we come into the expansive foyer. She is decidedly joyful, and the Motherhouse is more alive than any other time I've been here.

Built on the property of an historic estate in Fremont, the Motherhouse was finished in 1959, giving the Sisters a much needed larger, more modern home than the one they left in San Francisco. The Motherhouse is the residence of the current Congregational President and some of the Sisters, presently about a third of them. The other members are scattered throughout the United States, living in small groups or alone. Tonight, over one hundred Sisters, their families and friends crowd into the dining room for a celebration dinner and the anticipated entertainment.

Entertainment is an elaborate parody of the television show, *Wheel of Fortune*, featuring amusing contestants trying to guess messages appropriate for the occasion; interrupted by commercial breaks advertising such products as "The New Holy Ghost Pot." If I ever thought Sisters were aloof or sedate, tonight has disproved that idea.

Left: *Three Sisters pose as outrageously garbed contestants on "Wheel of Fortitude."*

These joyful, accomplished, religious women have dedicated their lives to God and to caring for other people. Wherever they are, whatever they are doing, all of their efforts are devoted to families and children, carrying on a tradition begun one hundred twenty-five years ago by their founders.

Right: *The Leadership Team members (Sisters Elaine Marie Sanchez, Sharon Flannigan, Teresa Marie Stiegler, and Martha Amezcua) participate in one of the skits.*

This book is a profile of them and their work, and a recognition of the contributions they made, and are continuing to make. Recognizing their charism is central to understanding who they are—this is the gift they have to share, it is what distinguishes them from other congregations, and draws new members to them—these are the family traits of Sisters of the Holy Family.

CHARISM AND QUALITIES OF SISTERS OF THE HOLY FAMILY

...the gifts they have to share

Ministers & Missionaries

Sister Elizabeth Murray brings a message of love and light to people in Hawaii.

Through their various ministries, in positions within the Church and at public and private agencies, Sisters of the Holy Family spread the joy of the gospel by word and example.

Missionaries at home. Not traveling to faraway lands, but serving the diverse cultures that make their home in the United States. Often working in small towns and rural areas. Frontier towns in Alaska, sugar plantations in Hawaii, remote ranching country in Utah and Nevada, the hill country of Kentucky, migrant settlements in California, ethnic neighborhoods in many large cities, all have missionaries from Sisters of the Holy Family.

With Open Hearts

Reaching out to people from all walks of life, they are especially drawn to people on the fringes, people who need special attention or extra care, people who are being forgotten or passed by in some way.

Sister Andrea Rangel is often found with her arms around children... encouraging...loving...teaching...sharing, like these children who are preparing for First Communion, whom she teaches in a bilingual class.

Innovative & Involved

Sister Kathy Littrell with two of her catechism students she involved in collecting food for the Second Harvest Food Bank, encouraging them to understand that service to others is part of being Christian.

Driven by a desire to get things done. More doers than philosophers, doing whatever is needed, never asking anyone else to do what they would not do, truly one with the people they serve. They are involved in all aspects of people's lives. A religious education teacher, who sees a poorly dressed child, will bring clothes to the family, and when finding a sick parent, will find help for health care. One gesture leads to another. Giving fully and completely, whatever is needed.

Caring & Hospitable

A friendly smile, a gentle hand on the arm, warm conversation.

The Sisters share a hospitality that extends beyond their own home. Wherever they are, they make people feel comfortable, welcome, included and important. They are the "someone who cares" that everyone needs. Giving...

sick people... comfort
grieving families... strength
the downcast... a sense of hope
children... security
the lonely... a reason for tomorrow
and everyone... a friend.

Sister Barbara Sheahan's warm smile is a welcome sight at the front door of many parishioners every day.

A few moments in the natural beauty and serene spirit of the Memorial Garden renews Sister Sharon Flannigan in a pause from a busy day.

Women of Hope

No matter what conditions they see, what poverty they walk among, what prejudice they encounter or what violence occurs; Sisters of the Holy Family remain women filled with hope. Buoyed by their belief in God and sustained by their spirituality, they remain hopeful for the future, hopeful for our society, country and humankind.

Sister Teresa Marie Stiegler in front of the newly installed peace pole, a symbol of the Sisters' dedication and involvement with a worldwide spirit to promote peace.

Advocates

Sisters of the Holy Family are advocates for families and children. At informal gatherings or large forums they speak out on issues that affect the people. They appear before city councils, serve on numerous boards in their communities, and network with other people and groups who are also working for justice. Always speaking for the needs of families and children.

leaners

Gleaners for God. Sisters of the Holy Family minister to small groups, often bringing people one at a time to God and Church. Going out and finding people who need them, they minister both by teaching and by how they live. The Sisters are a testament to God's love, showing each person they meet an unqualified love that comes from God.

Sister Cabrini Catania spends hours every week at the bedside of patients in hospitals, visiting and ministering.

Nomads

Many of the Sisters work away from permanent structures. They teach religious education in homes, work in neighborhoods, walk hospital hallways visiting people; in and out of buildings, up and down the highways, going where they feel needed. They go to the people, and when they see a need, they minister to it; maybe later they will have to worry about funding or how this fits some program. Frequently, once the program is established and has become strong they move on, knowing the people are taken care of. They go to find others in need.

Sister Judeana Davidson (right) leads a Women's Spirituality Workshop, encouraging women to reach beyond their past and explore new dimensions of themselves. Here, Sister Judeana and Karen McGregor read affirmations before casting them into the fire.

Feminists

From their earliest days, Sisters of the Holy Family have been pushing the barriers of what was considered the proper place of women. In the late 1800s, the Sisters went into rough neighborhoods of San Francisco to minister to the poor, where no "lady" would go. In the first part of the twentieth century, they were an uncommon sight driving their cars up and down the state. Today some members are at the forefront of expanding the role of women within the Catholic Church as they assume duties and roles that were once the exclusive responsibility of priests.

However, their strongest feminist actions are not for themselves, it is for others. Standing up for the rights of women, representing the ability of women to do whatever they choose, Sisters of the Holy Family work for the recognition of women's contributions to society and acknowledgment of the value of womanhood.

*S*piritual

Beyond being religious, they are spiritual and prayerful, having an inner peace which gives them both strength and gentleness. Communal prayer and worship unites them.

They draw on the spirituality of many cultures, and worship with people of many faiths. Prayer is woven into the tapestry of daily life.

Sister Helena Boss and Associate Linda Jozaitis Gill join hands and hearts in communal prayer.

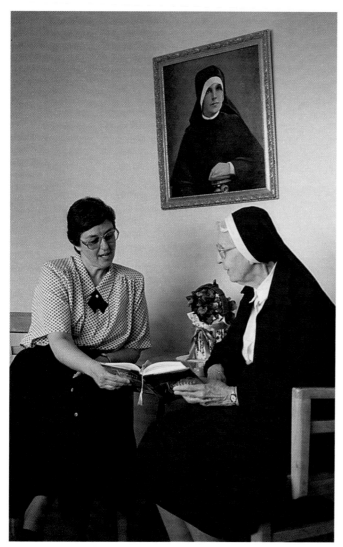

The past and present are blended together as Sisters Caritas Foster and Conception Graves share experiences and thoughts.

Contemporary

With a burning desire to be a vital part of a changing world, and yearning to find the best expression of their devotion to God and families, Sisters of the Holy Family have renewed themselves in the last 30 years. They have moved from an organization modeled in the 1870s to a contemporary organization. Together with other religious congregations they are creating a new model for religious life.

S isters

More than a title. This is their relationship with people. A sister. A person to share time with, laugh with and cry with. Sensing your need, they can be serious or lighthearted, insightful or supportive. They never hold themselves apart or above others. They are there for you. They love you. The kind of sister we all need; a companion on the journey of life.

Birth of a Sisterhood

Looking back at history, there is a tendency to believe that events were inevitable, which is rarely the case. It is only with bold individual action that change is effected. People regarded as heroes or leaders from the distance of time, frequently stood alone in their own time. History is made laboriously, without the luxury of knowing the outcome.

The birth of Sisters of the Holy Family (SHF) is the tale of four individuals whose separate paths all converged in San Francisco.

John Joseph Prendergast

As San Francisco was reeling from the incredible infusion of people seeking their fortunes in the Gold Rush, another ship tied up at her dock, bringing more people with dreams of making their fortunes. Among them, responding to a different call, was a newly ordained Irish priest, Father John Joseph Prendergast. The year was 1859.

Although he had heard that priests were desperately needed in this new frontier, he was not prepared for the amount of poverty and neglect he saw all around him. The city was exploding with growth, fortunes were made and lost within a few weeks, corruption and graft were commonplace in the city offices, and people were abandoned and lost amidst the confusion. With unbounded energy Father Prendergast threw himself into his work, even selling his own books and possessions to fund the charitable work he felt called to do.

His only frustration was how few he could care for among the vast numbers in the city that needed help, and he recognized a need for organized social relief work. He began to envision a congregation of religious women who would move throughout the city, not attached to any school or hospital, whose work would be to search out the poor and neglected, and provide for them whatever they needed. They would have to be strong and dedicated, filled with the love of God, in order to live for others in the same way he demanded of himself.

Elizabeth "Lizzie" Armer

Enticed by the gold fever to leave their home in Sydney, Australia, Robert Armer had brought his young family to California. Now he faced a heart wrenching decision. Although his work was in the mining camps, he realized he could not properly educate and provide for his three motherless children in that environment. So with his children's interests at heart, he approached his only acquaintances in San Francisco to ask their help. Richard and Mary Tobin graciously agreed to take the three children into their home. Although the boys eventually returned to be with their father in the mining camp, Elizabeth continued to live with the Tobins, and soon became an integral part of their large family.

As a member of the Tobin family, Lizzie lived in a fine home on Nob Hill. Richard Tobin, one of the founders and owners of Hibernia Bank, provided all the advantages for which any young girl could hope: a happy home with other children, a private education by the Presentation Sisters, a social life filled with music, parties and theater.

Mary Tobin frequently took Lizzie with her on visits to Mission Dolores and to help with various charities. When Lizzie grew older, they often talked about how to alleviate the suffering they saw, and they both sought practical ways to serve the poor.

Frequently Lizzie would stop and talk with the little children she saw on the streets. If she found them to be lacking religion, she would invite them to the house where she held catechism classes. Her pupils became so plentiful that, upon one occasion, Mr. Tobin complained Lizzie had turned their home into a kindergarten.

As much as she loved the Tobins and her life with them, within her heart Lizzie sensed she was being called to serve God. She felt drawn to enter a cloistered community where she could devote her life to prayer and service. Not sure how to proceed, she went to see the Archbishop to ask his permission to enter a convent.

Archbishop Joseph Sadoc Alemany, O.P.

A Dominican missionary, Father Joseph Alemany had been persecuted by the government before leaving his Spanish homeland, and had been serving the poor in Ohio, Tennessee and Kentucky for nine years before he arrived in California. He was appointed Bishop of Monterey in 1850, with responsibilities for Northern California, Nevada, Baja California and other Western territories—a huge area. On his first tour around San Francisco, realizing the enormous amount of work to be done just within the city, he decided to move from Monterey and establish his headquarters in San Francisco, the active center of the territory, so that he could devote his energies more efficiently to the people.

Many miners, having given up on finding gold, had come to San Francisco to start another life, and their families were beginning to arrive. This raucous, wild frontier town needed to be civilized if it was going to be a home for families. Bishop Alemany quickly began bringing to California orders of sisters to staff hospitals and schools. From seminaries in Europe and the Eastern United States he requested priests to serve the burgeoning population of Catholics in his frontier diocese. Father Prendergast was one who answered his plea.

Many religious communities of men and women also responded to his call for help. They established hospitals, schools, orphanages, homes for unwed mothers. During emergencies, like the smallpox epidemic which threatened to wipe out large segments of the population in 1868, these dedicated religious, along with many ordinary citizens, would put aside their regular duties and come to the aid of needy families and patients throughout the city.

However, beyond emergencies, there was no organization actively searching out and caring for the hidden poor who were outside the boundaries of Catholic institutions. Recognizing the need for such work led to Father Prendergast's vision for a new order of religious women. These women would not have other duties, but be devoted entirely to seeking and finding people who needed help, and to giving religious training to children who could not attend the Catholic schools. Eventually he shared his vision with Archbishop Alemany whose mission matched his. So, on the day when Lizzie Armer came to request the Archbishop's permission to enter a cloister, he answered, "Father Prendergast and I have another work for you to do."

A second young woman (who later decided not to continue) initially joined Lizzie in her work. With the blessings of the church and their families, on November 6, 1872 they moved into a small flat on San Francisco's Pine Street, rented for them by Mrs. Tobin. There, they began to devote themselves to the service of the poor. This was the inauspicious birth of Sisters of the Holy Family.

Ellen O'Connor

About the same time, across town was another woman considering her future.

With her parents, she had crossed the country from Boston to California in a covered wagon when she was only three and had lived in a mining camp in El Dorado County. Even amidst the wildness of their surroundings, her parents had provided Ellen O'Connor with the same stable and religious up-bringing she would have had if they stayed in Boston. They were faithful Catholics, and Ellen was delighted when they would travel down the winding mountain roads to the nearest church and she was allowed to assist at Mass.

When the family moved to San Francisco, Ellen attended parochial schools, studying with Sisters of Charity and the Dominican Sisters. It was because she so admired them and their lives that she wanted to become a sister. When she confided her desire to Father Andrew Cullen, asking him to direct her choice between these religious orders, he surprised her by saying, "If I were you I should try this new work which Father Prendergast is starting."

It was now the spring of 1874, a year and a half since Lizzie had started her work. Two different women had joined her for short periods, but neither one stayed, so she continued alone. People had begun to deride her lofty idea of a new religious order. Two people remained her staunch supporters, Mrs. Tobin and Father Prendergast. Therefore, on the day when Ellen O'Connor knocked on her door, Lizzie asked with some sense of apprehension. "Have you come to stay?" Hearing a confident "I hope so." Lizzie took her hand and exclaimed, "you are my birthday gift!"

Now there were two, and the beginning of a sisterhood.

Gradually they were joined by other women. They were not yet a religious community, simply women devoting their lives to God and the poor. They had no religious training, and had not made a novitiate. What they did have was dedication and zeal for their work, and a wonderful companionship among themselves.

In 1878, Ellen O'Connor was the first to complete a year of novitiate, having been sent by Archbishop Alemany to study with the Dominican Sisters at their Benicia Convent. Therefore, when she took her religious vows and assumed the name of Sister Mary Teresa of Jesus, she also became the first Superior of Holy Family Sisters.

On the Feast of St. Joseph in 1880, Lizzie and four other women made their vows and joined Sister Teresa as religious women in their new convent. Having now completed her novitiate, Lizzie was appointed by Archbishop Alemany to serve as Superior, a position she would hold for 25 years.

Father Prendergast and Lizzie Armer's dream had come true. The Sisters' work encompassed a wide variety of activities: dispensing food and clothing to the poor, instructing children in religion, nursing the sick at home, providing day care, teaching sewing and cooking classes, caring for and decorating the cathedral, home visiting, and giving encouragement and friendship to families throughout the city.

Like the first six Sisters, for 125 years others have joined Sisters of the Holy Family possessed by a desire to serve both God and humanity. Their mission continues to be in service to families and children, and they continue to go to the people, wherever they are. Their spirits are modeled after the spirits of the first Sisters; however, as an organization they continue to evolve, always answering contemporary needs in society.

The Leaders of
Sisters of the Holy Family
the first 125 years
1872-1997

Without vision, nothing new is begun; without leadership, nothing will continue.

For their collective and individual contributions, we honor the ten women who led Sisters of the Holy Family during their first 125 years.

Superior
Sister M. Dolores Armer
1880-1905

- *Foundress*
- *Unwavering dedication to her dream*
- *Gave freely and completely to others*
- *Charismatic leader who inspired followers*

Superior
Sister M. Teresa O'Connor
1878-1880 & 1905-1921

- *Co-foundress and first novice directress*
- *Great reverence for God and the Church*
- *Persistent solicitor of funds from benefactors*
- *Began the SHF expansion beyond San Francisco*

Superior
Sister M. Gertrude Rourke
1921-1925

- *The bridge between the foundresses and the continuum of SHF*
- *Organized the 50th Jubilee celebration*
- *Chronicler of history and memoirs of Sisters Dolores & Teresa*

History is judged from a distance, individuals are valued moment to moment as they live. Many small things done well are just as important as doing one big thing.

**Mother General
Sister Consilio Casey
1925-1940**

- *Youngest president, her election had to be approved by the Bishop because of her youth*
- *Began the process to receive Pontifical approval*

**Mother General
Sister Celestine Delehanty
1940-1952**

- *Dedicated to spreading the Gospel*
- *Encouraged academic foundations for Sisters' ministries*
- *Opened many houses around California*

**Mother General
Sister Perpetua McCarthy
1952-1964**

- *Devoted to memory of Sister Dolores and her work*
- *Received Pontifical recognition of the work of SHF*
- *Accomplished funding for and moving to the new Motherhouse in Fremont*

**Mother/Superior General
Sister Maureen Hennessey
1964-1975**

- *Presided over Chapter of Adaptation, and initiated implementation of Vatican II*
- *Initiated the process of renewal*
- *Orchestrated the centennial celebration*

Elected leaders are both a reflection of those they lead, and an inspiration of what they should be.

Their fate and success are inescapably intertwined.

**Superior General
Sister Margaret Mary Nelligan
1975-1983**
- *Implemented modernization of SHF, including changes in internal structure*
- *Encouraged individual choice and responsibility*

**President
Sister Karen Stern
1983-1991**
- *Completed new SHF Constitutions*
- *Encouraged Sisters to move into leadership roles in diocesan offices, and elsewhere*
- *Associate Program began under her direction*

**President
Sister Elaine Marie Sanchez
1991-present**
- *Implemented concept of Leadership Team*
- *Networked SHF with other social and religious groups to expand opportunities for services and effect change*
- *Advocate for social justice issues*

It is a blessing to be graced with the right leader; one who can both build on the past and break away from it.

Ministries

One Charism
...Many Ministries
Journey with me
to meet twenty-five
Sisters of the Holy Family,
each involved in a different ministry,
yet each continuing
a tradition from the past.

•

Missionaries at Home
Caring for Families and Children
On the Road
Teachers Outside of Schools
Serving Special People
Hospitality of the Heart

"There are hearts to heal, and souls to save in our busy city streets. This is the work God wants you to do."

Archbishop Joseph S. Alemany

Missionaries at Home

Not traveling to foreign countries, Sisters of the Holy Family are missionaries at home to the myriad of people from many cultures who come to America. From their earliest beginnings, Sisters of the Holy Family reached out to minorities and the poor.

In the 1920s the Sisters began to spread beyond the San Francisco area. Spruce Hill was one area of Los Angeles where they ministered for many years to the large immigrant population.

Sister Maria Lucia Nieto, originally from the Central Valley of California, returned there to teach the children of the Mexican farm laborers. She was the first of a long list of Sisters to minister to the Spanish speaking community. For many years, every summer the Sisters went to small rural communities like Hanford when the laborers returned to work the fields.

HAWAII

In 1947, six Sisters were sent to Honokaa, Hawaii as missionaries. Courage and faith kept them going through many lonely and challenging days in their first few years. Standing outside their convent are Sisters Alphonsus, Dorothea, Damian, Rosemary, Bernardine, and M. Brendan (later known as Brenda Marie) with Bishop Sweeney.

Hawaii was a five day voyage by ship from San Francisco and when the Sisters left California they did not know where they would live or exactly where they would be working, just that the Bishop had requested they come to teach catechism.

Although the Catholic Church had been in Hawaii for many years, there was very little religious education, only Mass on Sundays. Just as they had done in California, the Sisters went out to all the surrounding towns and started classes. The next spring hundreds of their pupils received First Communion.

(photos left to right)
Catechism classes were held outdoors, or wherever they found space.
The Virgin Mary receives a coronation of leis on May Day.
Mother Perpetua visits the City of Refuge in Honaunau, Kona, 1953.
Wisemen, Hawaiian style, ready for a Christmas pageant.

TEXAS

With no place to hold Summer School in San Antonio, Texas in the 1950s, the Sisters found someone to loan them a vacant lot. There, each summer for several years, they set up what became known as Tent City. Children arrived by the truckload, brought in from outlying ranches and the barrios.

NEVADA

These Navajo girls, outside Corpus Christi Church in Stewart, Nevada, were studying in preparation for Confirmation with Sisters of the Holy Family who brought the first catechism classes to this remote area in 1935.

Frontier Pastor

Sister Marie Ann Brent
Pastoral Administrator, St Francis Xavier • Valdez, Alaska

Biting wind blows piles of snow against the building, the temperature hovers at minus thirty degrees, daylight will last for only a few hours. Here, in this last frontier of the United States, Sister Marie Ann Brent continues the missionary tradition of Sisters of the Holy Family.

Inside the church, Sister Marie Ann is presiding at one of the three Eucharistic Services she conducts each week. If this were summer, there would be visitors in the pews, and she would have started the service with her customary introduction, designed to answer the unspoken questions of people surprised to see a woman at the front of the church. "I am Sister Marie Ann Brent, the Pastoral Administrator at St. Francis Xavier. We are without a priest in this parish. The service you will be part of today is called a Eucharistic Service and is very much like other services you attend." But this is winter, so everyone here knows her and respects her as their religious leader. She has been with them since 1993, asked by Archbishop Hurley to come to Valdez because the people needed a nurturing pastoral guidance that he knew was her special gift.

Sister Marie Ann was the first pastoral administrator in Alaska. St. Francis Xavier is her third parish. Now there are eight sisters from other congregations who are also pastoral administrators in the Archdiocese of Anchorage. Basically they do almost everything a pastor would do. A visiting priest comes twice a month, celebrates Mass and provides them with sufficient "hosts" for their other services. The rest of the time, the sister is the pastor and is part of the cutting edge for women in the Catholic Church. As the Church searches for ways to provide for their people, and there continues to be a shortage of priests, the lines of distinction between what a priest can do and what a sister, as a pastoral administrator, can do are blurring. Sister Marie Ann and the other pastoral administrators in Alaska give Communion, baptize and, in special circumstances, witness marriages.

Contributed photo. Photographer unknown.

Becoming part of the Alaskan community includes pleasures like fishing on Yakutat Bay. This day, when she caught six salmon, she calls the "happiest day of my life!"

But Sister Marie Ann is not content to just serve within the confines of the Church's walls, she carries her ministry into the community. She is an Emergency Medical Technician and a Hospital Chaplain; two positions that allow her to serve people beyond her parish.

Sometimes the ministries become intertwined. "One day there was a small plane crash with two local men aboard. I went out as part of the Emergency Medical Team, but when we arrived it was pretty apparent they were beyond medical care. It was gruesome and they were trying to keep people back, but I noticed, in the crowd, a couple from my parish who were really distraught. When I knew my help was no longer needed as an EMT, I asked to be excused from the team and went over to the couple. They told me one of the deceased was a young man from Norway whom they had sort of adopted. I was able to provide pastoral comfort for them at their moment of greatest need. Later the woman asked me to put together a non-denominational Memorial Service for both men which was attended by the whole community. This is the kind of ministry I am most excited about, and is so typical in Alaska—service to the whole person."

Sister Marie Ann first came to Alaska in 1970 when Archbishop Hurley asked the San Francisco Archdiocese for volunteers to come with him for six weeks to teach religious education in the summer. Within a couple of weeks she knew that this was where she belonged. She loved the people, the frontier feeling, the phenomenon of Alaska. In 1973, she returned to Alaska full time with Sister Victor Negrete, SHF. They ministered to three logging camps and two native villages. Then in 1979, Sister Marie Ann went with Sister Marian McNamee, SHF, to the Aleutian Islands, where they were the first Catholic contact for the people in 35 years. The more remote and undeveloped, the more she liked it. Tiny towns, "not citified with streets and sidewalks," such as Dutch Harbor, a fishing port accessed only by air or water, and Dillingham, a small Eskimo village in the Southwestern Alaskan cold belt, became her home. Sister Marie Ann says "I love going out to the native villages and the one-on-one work in these small communities. I always knew a nine-to-five job was not for me. I went to Catholic schools, so I knew sisters taught, then one day I saw a picture of a nun out in the field with children and I thought 'Wow! To go out where there is no formal structure. That is what I want to do.' When I went to Texas for two years, I thought that was the closest I would get to real mission work. Little did I know that I would get to come to Alaska."

On the cutting edge for women in the Catholic Church …doing everything a priest would do, except administer sacraments.

When she talks about Alaska and her ministry, her face lights up. She speaks in a round articulated voice that is soothing. It is easy to see why people look to her for guidance and comfort, and why Archbishop Hurley asked her to come to St. Francis Xavier to provide healing to a parish that had experienced many crises in the recent past. She has been the leader they needed, and the community has become revitalized under her guidance. When her work is done here, Sister Marie Ann hopes to go to another small community in the Alaska frontier, the smaller the better. She is definitely a pioneer woman, happiest in conditions the rest of us might call primitive, and devoted to her ministry with the Alaskan people.

Making the Story Live

Sister Michaela O'Connor
Parish Sister to the Kmhmu' • Richmond, California

Tonight is December 21st, a dozen people have gathered in a small apartment for a Christmas prayer service. Conversation is in three languages: Laotian, English and Kmhmu' (pronounced: ka moo'). As new immigrants to the United States these Kmhmu', originally from the hill country in what is now Laos, are part of a tiny minority in the United States; perhaps only 3000 in the entire country. Like many immigrants, they came here to make a better life for their families and to escape persecution at home. Because they are such a small group there are no social services specifically for them, and very few non-Kmhmu' can even speak their language, but they are a communal people and they take care of each other. In Richmond, California (the largest concentration of Kmhmu' in the USA) they are also taken care of by Sister Michaela O'Connor and Father Don MacKinnon, CSSR, who have adopted the Kmhmu' as their special mission.

They don't have a church of their own. So, like tonight, many of their gatherings are in homes. Sister Michaela has learned some Kmhmu' from them, some of them have learned English, and they sometimes switch to Laotian, the official language in their country and the only one allowed to be spoken in their schools.

Sister Michaela tells the Christmas Story in contemporary words, with emotion, laughter, pantomime, and an incredibly expressive face.

Sister Michaela is their Parish Sister, which means she does whatever she sees that they need. She teaches religious education, plans holiday events, visits the sick, helps them find jobs, enrolls them in English classes, explains the ways of their new country, encourages, nurtures and comforts. What she loves most is sharing the story of Jesus. To people who have little material possessions, she offers a gift of the incredible wonder of God's love. Her special gift is bringing this story alive through her wonderful talent as storyteller.

Seated on the floor, Sister Michaela begins tonight's service, leading everyone in singing "Our Father", and then in a very personal prayer for the people gathered in the room, remembering all their families...a mother in the hospital with a bad heart...a sister in Georgia whose husband has left her...two daughters who suffer from seizures...a sister in Laos whose rice crop was ruined by the rains...and everyone who is in need, especially the homeless who need a place to stay like Mary and Joseph. Thus, Sister Michaela begins to tell the Christmas story, a story I know well, a story I could tell; but it is as if this were a new story. I am enthralled, as is everyone in the room.

In this small apartment we share the same wonder as the shepherds did two thousand years ago.

"How tired Mary and Joseph must be, traveling for days, and Mary is very pregnant." Sister Michaela looks at the women, "You all know how uncomfortable you were before your babies were born. And Mary has to ride a donkey across rough terrain! It is hot and dusty. Joseph is doing everything he can to take care of her, but she is very tired. The government required that they take this trip, to be counted in the census. When they finally reach Bethlehem, Joseph goes door to door. Knock, knock...'Go away, go away.' He can't find a room anywhere. In desperation, Joseph finally begs one innkeeper 'there must be some place we can lie down, we'll take anything. It is not for myself—look at my wife, she needs rest.' 'Well, there's the stable, but it's messy and smelly.' 'We'll take it!' Joseph exclaims and helps Mary off the donkey, leaving her to rest sitting against the side of the building while he goes to the stable. It is smelly and dirty, but he cleans away the dirt, moves the animals to the side, finds new straw and prepares a bed for her."

Sister Michaela pauses frequently for one of the women to translate. As Sister talks, the women nod and murmur, sympathizing, even stopping her to ask questions about how the census worked: they ask if Joseph and Mary had to pay Bethlehem a fee for having the baby there, like they did in Laos, kind of a "new head tax." When we reach the point in the story where Baby Jesus is born there are murmurs of delight. I have been quietly taking pictures, now as Sister Michaela begins to talk about the shepherds, I reach for my flash. When she says "and a star appeared" I produce a flash of light. We're all thrilled. In this small apartment we share the same wonder as the shepherds did two thousand years ago.

The evening ends with Christmas carols—taking turns singing for each other in our own languages, Laotian, Kmhmu' and English; and finally all three languages are blended together singing a French carol "Divine Enfant."

En Español

Sister Jo Marie Arredondo
Mexican American Cultural Center, Activities Coordinator • San Antonio, Texas

Inside a red brick building, that looks like an old high school, 30 people are gathering in a large lounge. All the conversation is in Spanish, which is not unusual in San Antonio, Texas, except that almost no one in the room looks Hispanic. I see mostly middle-aged Anglo-Saxons, but I hear fluent Spanish. They have been studying, eating, breathing, talking and even dreaming in Spanish for several weeks here, at the Mexican American Cultural Center.

Mexican Americans are over 20 percent of the Catholic population in America, and the majority of Catholics in many areas. In spite of their large presence, historically their culture has not been embraced by the Church in America. Recently that is changing, and Sister Jo Marie Arredondo is one of a group of religious leaders helping to bring about the change.

Sister Jo Marie works at the Mexican American Cultural Center in San Antonio Texas, whose purpose is to teach Mexican American culture and language, as distinct from Spanish. People come from all over the world to attend the Center's courses and workshops. Most of the students are priests or sisters, some are religious leaders from other churches. Sister Jo Marie first worked at the Center from 1980-1983 developing some of the classes. She returned in 1991 to offer a new dimension to the students' experience, helping them develop an understanding of the Mexican American culture through activities outside of the classroom, and through prayers and liturgies. She believes if the students want to be effective religious leaders with their Mexican American parishioners, they need to do more than learn the language, she wants them to appreciate the unique values, the lifestyle and the traditions of Mexican Americans.

Her most important role is to stretch minds, to help the students see the world through a Mexican American's eyes.

To do that, Sister Jo Marie arranges for weekly field trips, using San Antonio as their classroom, attending grassroots political meetings in the neighborhoods, or participating in religious celebrations, like Las Posadas, unique to Mexican Americans. She is also the advisor for planning the daily morning prayer service and evening Mass, which the students conduct in Spanish as part of their curriculum. Her most important role is to stretch minds, to help the students see the world through a Mexican American's eyes.

Roberto Piña, one of the other instructors, says of Sister Jo Marie, "she is one of the most creative people I know...always thinking of new ways to do things. She is constantly raising our consciousness regarding Mexican Americans and other minorities by helping us look at things in new ways."

Gathered for a farewell party, MACC students sing Mexican hymns taught them by Sister Jo Marie (on left). In a few weeks, these songs will be repeated in parishes across the United States as the students incorporate them into their own services. Father Paschal Cacavalle (on right), a Franciscan Capuchin priest, had been in the Bronx for years when his diocese asked him to go to Patterson, New Jersey to serve in a Hispanic parish. Because it had been decades since he studied Spanish in high school, Father Cacavalle attended MACC for an in-depth Spanish language course a few months ago. Now he is back taking the Pastoral course to help him incorporate more of the Mexican American culture into his work. "Knowing the language isn't enough, it is just a first step, I needed to understand their culture and religious heritage. I don't know of any other place where I could have gone to learn what they teach here."

Giving them Voice

Sister Mary Lange
Coordinator of Lay Ministry Training &
Liturgy Chairperson for the Island of Hawaii

When I first meet her, Sister Mary Lange seems very different from Sister Jo Marie, one is crisp and quick, the other soft and deliberate, but as Sister Mary talks I realize the mission for both women is the same: to increase awareness and appreciation of a special culture.

Sister Mary Lange has two positions with the Diocese of Honolulu. One aspect of her ministry is to work with people throughout the diocese, helping plan liturgical celebrations. Her focus is to make the worship more meaningful to people. One group she has worked with are the native Hawaiians, who are now a minority in their own land. "Historically the church has not always addressed the needs of native people, but we are trying to change. One way is by inculturation of the liturgy to the host culture. [Allowing local culture to shape the celebration.] The changes we are making are small, but significant. For instance in the Polynesian culture, people always sit when they listen to someone they respect or revere, so in some of our parishes we sit rather than stand during the reading of the gospel." She recognizes that many Hawaiians participate in both traditional native ceremonies and their Catholic religion, seeing no conflict between them; performing dances in honor of Pele, the goddess of fire, whom they view as one aspect of our God. Constantly finding ways to integrate native traditions into church services—particularly music, blessings and hospitality, which are so important to the Hawaiians—Sister Mary Lange is an advocate for the Hawaiian people within the Church.

Historically the church has not always addressed the needs of native people, but we are trying to change.

She is also an advocate for them in their fight for sovereignty. Like the Native Americans, the Hawaiians had their land taken from them by the United States government, they were given many promises which were never kept. Now they are struggling to have the promises met, and to establish a "Nation within a Nation" similar to the Native Americans'. The first step is to be recognized as the native people of Hawaii which, to date, the federal government has not done. Sister Mary, along with many others, is working with the people to increase their voice and power.

Sister Mary Lange was Minister of Ceremony at the reinternment of Blessed Damien of Moloku'i at Kalawao in 1995. For the Hawaiians this "coming home of Father Damien" was a very important event, which was commemorated with many celebrations. Each island planned and hosted services and events in honor of this Belgian priest and his ministry to the lepers of the Hawaiian islands.

To this effort, Sister Mary Lange brings her ability to look at the big picture, to analyze, plan and organize.

These are the same gifts she uses in her other role as coordinator of Lay Ministry Training, setting up a variety of educational opportunities. "As the Church is reaching out to people, increasingly trying to involve the laity in the processes of the Church, it is necessary to provide them with the skills they need. Training people to do whatever they are called to do within the Church is my role." She speaks with great enthusiasm for her work, and love for the Hawaiian people. "Lay ministry is important in all parishes, but it is particularly important here. We need to help the people feel a sense of ownership about their religion and the Church."

"The purpose of this Sisterhood may indeed be found in its name: 'The Holy Family'."

Father John Prendergast

Caring for Families & Children

The mission of Sisters of the Holy Family is to serve families and children. The family being the world's first and holiest institution, and the home, the foundation of our society, the Sisters dedicate themselves to strengthen and enrich the family, and to nurture children.

Day Homes

Archbishop Alemany became concerned about the children of working parents he saw during his tours around San Francisco. Working mothers had no safe place to leave their children and would often leave toddlers in the care of siblings, only slightly older themselves.

Pictured in St. Mary's Day Home (one of the Sisters' Day Homes in San Francisco) is the Kindergarten Morning Ring, what the Sisters called "the most precious hour of the day."

As soon as there were enough women in the Holy Family community, the Archbishop persuaded them to find a suitable house and begin caring for young children. When their first Day Home was started in 1878 with fourteen students, it was the only institution of its kind in San Francisco. It was so successful, they soon outgrew the house on Post Street, and the Sisters found themselves expanding to larger or new quarters every few years. St. Francis Day Home was established in 1881, and within a few years, the Sisters were operating three Day Homes in San Francisco. From the beginning, what distinguished their Day Homes was the quality of care lavished on the children. Clean clothes, pleasant surroundings, loving guidance, nourishing food, learning and fun activities were offered to the children whose homes were often quite meager by comparison.

When the 1906 Earthquake destroyed all three of the Sisters' Day Homes in San Francisco, they moved to the tent cities which became home for thousands of people. Here they cared for as many children as needed them, and helped with other relief work for families. They organized sewing classes and supervised the making of thousands of dresses and aprons each month, which were given away to whomever was in need of clothes.

While re-building their Day Homes in San Francisco, Sisters of the Holy Family established St. Elizabeth's Day Home in San Jose in 1907, and St. Vincent's Day Home in Oakland in 1911, both of which are still in operation today. A report from 1918 documents that the Sisters were caring for over 1700 children each day in the three cities combined, "...caring for them with the tender charity of a Christian mother."

Caring for children included providing medicine and food both within the Day Homes and to children and families wherever they found them.

The Sisters organized basketball teams for the boys, and Brownie troops for the girls, like this one from St. Genevieve's parish in Fresno, pictured during a visit with the Brownies from Blessed Sacrament Parish.

Today they continue to find new ways to enrich the lives of children and preserve and protect families.

Second Best Place in the World

Holy Family, San Francisco • St. Elizabeth's, San Jose • St. Vincent's, Oakland

A place to play...to learn...to grow. A safe and secure place, where there is always someone to care for and protect children. A place filled with love and laughter and friends. This is a home, a special kind of home, a Day Home.

Holy Family, St. Elizabeth's and St. Vincent's Day Homes all continue to provide this special kind of place for children which the Sisters of the Holy Family envisioned when they started them. "We prepare this place for the children. They are our guests. We want them to feel like this is a second home for them, to feel comfortable here, to be proud of it. We want it to be the second best place in the world for a child (after their own home)," explains Corinne Marie Mohrmann, Executive Director of St. Vincent's.

Each home has developed its own uniqueness over the years. Each is run by its own Director and Board, but they all remain true to the spirit of the Holy Family. They are dedicated to providing a nurturing environment for children of working parents. In addition, they offer other services for the families of their children; from job training to parenting classes, providing resources for medical help, housing and drug rehabilitation.

Children arrive at St. Vincent's in Oakland.

52

Each Day Home cares for over a hundred children every day, grouping them into classes based on their individual development. Days are filled with a variety of structured and spontaneous activities, group participation and independent play. There is social time, quiet time, nap time, play time, lesson time and story time.

Many of these children's parents are struggling to provide a home in a hostile urban environment, and life at home may be less than ideal. The Day Homes provide needed stability. Here, children receive individual attention, are stimulated, nurtured and encouraged.

The goal is to prepare them for life, to give them self-esteem, and to teach them skills and values that will be a foundation for their future. The teachers, all certified in Early Childhood Education, tailor the activities to the abilities and development of each child.

Simple lessons are woven into play. Sister Ann Maureen Murphy, Executive Director of Holy Family Day Home, talks with this group of three-year olds about colors and shapes and healthy food.

Coloring, pasting, practicing their letters and numbers are part of everyday activities. At St. Elizabeth's, the students enjoy weekly classes in the Art Barn where they develop motor skills, self-confidence and creativity through arts and crafts projects.

Lessons include activities as simple as brushing teeth, and as exciting as using the computer; equally needed in today's world.

Wonderful playgrounds are part of the Day Homes. There are swings and sand boxes, structures to climb on and crawl through. There are gardens to dig in and fruit to be picked. Physical activity is a vital part of the program, which is dedicated to developing the heart and mind and body of every child.

Such playful surroundings do not just happen, they are the result of years of work. Today's staff is building on the traditions of yesterday's Sisters. The Day Homes are special because the caring is special. Although the staff is no longer just Sisters, they all share the same values and caring for children.

Sister Adrienne Andreani, the Health and Nutrition Director at St. Vincent's, and also the resident patron of animals, always has a family of gerbils or rabbits for the children to play with and learn to care for...teaching them to love as they are loved.

Sister Adrienne Andreani is the resident patron of animals at St. Vincent's.

55

"One more push," the kids plead, and, of course, Sister Marianne Smith obliges. She is 71 years old and returned to Holy Family Day Home four years ago, because she was not yet ready to retire. She first worked here almost 50 years ago, and remembers Sister Ann Maureen, now Executive Director, coming to the Day Home as a child.

The Sisters are not the only ones to return to the Homes. Several of the children are second or third generation enrollees, and their parents are proud to share this experience with their children.

Recently, a man walked in Holy Family's front door with an envelope in his hand. He said he attended the Day Home in 1932, and last month when he was at his mother's side before she died, she said "Remember the Day Home." With that, he gave them a generous check. After taking a tour of the Home, he left, having rekindled memories of his childhood. Two weeks later he returned with another check in renewed appreciation of their continuing work.

For the Directors, fund-raising is a major part of their job. Parents' fees and limited government funding pay only a portion of the costs; private donations must make up the balance. Both Sister Ann Maureen Murphy, at Holy Family, and Corinne Marie Mohrmann, at St Vincent's, are embarked on ambitious programs to build their endowment funds, which will insure the continuation of the Day Homes, with less reliance on the vagrancies of the political climate.

Our Kids Deserve the Best

Sister Diane Maguire and Sister Marie Julie Casattas
Variety Day Home • Las Vegas, Nevada

Tonight is a United Way Campaign kickoff event in Las Vegas, and many of the influential business people in town are in attendance. So is Sister Diane Maguire. This is just one of many community gatherings she will attend this month. Networking, forming relationships, is important for her. Tonight she meets the Public Relations Manager of the new MGM.

When he learns about her work, he cordially says "Let me know if I can do anything to help." She's ready, "I'd like 200 plastic champagne buckets. We'll use them to store each child's personal blanket." He has just learned what many of the other leaders in town already know, Sister Diane will give him plenty of opportunities to support her Day Home.

During a moment away from administration, Sister Diane plays with toddlers.

Champagne buckets to store blankets is a typical Sister Diane innovation. State law mandated that each child's blanket be stored separately, and not in a locker or drawer with the child's other possessions. Plastic champagne buckets seemed the perfect solution—lightweight, washable, the right size, and available just by asking. The Variety Day Home is filled with contributions that Sister Diane has asked for: carpeting from The Golden Nugget, flooring from Donald W. Reynolds Foundation, cribs and blinds from the Walters Group, chests of drawers from Hacienda Hotel and Sam's Town. Other businesses provide services she needs, like Davey Tree Service who brought in a crew of men for a day to spray, plant, trim trees and do other playground maintenance. Sister Diane is not hesitant to ask. "You have to have guts. I just ask for what I need, and don't let up. I don't give a darn how much runaround I get, I'm not asking for myself, it's for the kids. I just keep asking till we get what we need...and I don't want junk. Our kids deserve the best."

Sister Marie Julie Casattas joins the teacher and children in one classroom as they sing a song about their bodies.

When she solicits for the Day Home, Sister Diane believes she is doing more than helping the disadvantaged children, she is also ministering to the people from whom she is soliciting. "We are helping them fulfill their Christian duty to minister to someone else and to care about others." When she looks at you with her sharp blue eyes, and tells you what she needs, it would be difficult to refuse.

The Variety Day Home is a testament to the ingenuity of Sister Diane. It was the first modern Las Vegas Day Home to accept infants and is looked to as a model and national leader of infant and toddler care. I spend an afternoon there, talking to Sister Diane and her staff, watching their work with the children. There are over 200 children, ages four months to six years in a sprawling one story building in a poor neighborhood. From the outside it is quite unassuming and plain, but the inside is filled with life and color and love.

"What we are doing needs to be repeated many times, in every city. There is a great need for affordable day care in our country, and we need to address it if we hope to get people off welfare."

Sister Marie Julie Casattas, another member of Sisters of the Holy Family, starts each morning at a desk near the front door, greeting each child and parent as they arrive, and logging them into the computer. Logging in and out is part of an elaborate security and record keeping system maintained for each child. Most of the children at Variety Day Home are from low income households, the parents must be employed or going to school, and trying to take responsibility for their children. Everyone pays a fee, depending on their income, but with fees starting as low as $3.25 per week, the bulk of the operating money comes from other sources. Currently the Day Home has seven different sources, each with its own rules about who qualifies, how the money can be spent, and how it must be accounted for. It is a huge administrative task to maintain current records, keep the required reports going out and the funding coming in, but Sister Diane says it is much easier now that they have the computer to track the necessary information for each grant. "And it is worth whatever we have to do to provide for these children."

The children obviously love the place. When we walk onto the playground, 30 four-year olds swarm around Sister Diane, calling out her name, telling her about their day. She sits down on a cement block and leads them in singing "The people on the bus go up and down..."

They all move up and down with the song, and at the end break into peals of laughter. In one of the classrooms they are having story hour; in another they are playing, individually and in small groups, with blocks and dolls and fire trucks. How much of the time is structured depends on the age of the children, but even in play they are being taught. I hear one teacher encouraging two children to share, another is showing a child how to tie a shoe.

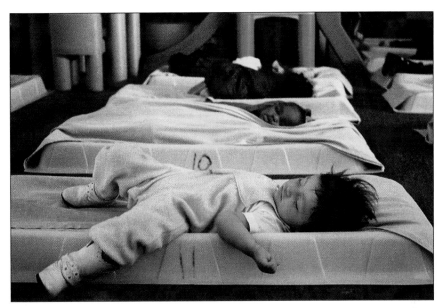

We peek in one room where 15 two-year olds are absolutely quiet ...it's nap time.

Finally Sister Diane takes us to a nursery. This is her pride and joy. Before their Day Home started accepting infants in 1982 there was no day care in Las Vegas for children until they were potty trained. "Without child care, parents can't work. What we are doing needs to be repeated many times, in every city. There is a great need for affordable day care in our country, and we need to address it if we hope to get people off welfare." The nursery is ringed with cribs, the lights are subdued. Some children are napping, a few are being rocked, others are playing quietly. There are three attendants in here. It takes a lot of care for infants—changing diapers, feeding, playing, loving. Imagine a room with seven children in high chairs, learning to feed themselves!

The Variety Day Home children are lucky, this is the kind of nurturing environment every child needs. These are childhood days filled with play, naps, lunch, stories, outside games, running and laughter. The staff hopes that the foundation they are giving the children will help them grow into responsible adults, but they also know that won't always happen. There are many other forces which will affect the children's development and future. Nonetheless, it is their mission to start the children out right.

So Sister Diane works eleven hours a day, providing for the children and overseeing her staff of fifty. She requires all of her teachers to have CDA (Child Development Associate) credentials, well beyond what is required by the state. On the day I visited, she was also training teachers from other child care centers and the Clark County School District, who were working towards their accreditation. The Day Home offers instruction both as a lab school, and through a series of video tapes on Early Childhood Teaching.

There seems to be no end to Sister Diane's energy. She is an amazing woman of action, enterprise and innovation.

In Times of Crisis

Sister Martha Amezcua
Child Welfare Worker • Alameda County, California

The phone rings, a teacher is calling to report that one of her students frequently has unexplainable bruises. To the woman who answers the phone this is, unfortunately, a typical call. The Hot Line at the Alameda County Children and Family Services receives over a hundred calls like it a day. This is the front line in child protection in California, where doctors, teachers and other social service providers are required to report any circumstances that might indicate a child is endangered or abused.

This case is assigned to Sister Martha Amezcua, one of the 22 child welfare workers in the county. Within the next two days she will investigate the situation, determine whether there is a problem, and decide what action needs to be taken. "We almost always visit the home. It allows us to see all the circumstances that affect the child. It is also the best intervention—telling a parent that someone else cares about their children; it is a wake-up call, and sometimes that is enough." She will decide if the child should be removed from the home or what can be done to help maintain the family. The goal is to keep families out of the justice system whenever possible; instead, to put them in contact with resources to help them.

Sister Martha explains that the issue, or problem, is not whether parents love their children; most do. The issue is whether they are being good parents. "We aren't talking about being perfect parents—

Sister Martha goes over the information for a new case with a co-worker.

just adequate, providing for the physical needs of their children, protecting them, not abusing them. It is amazing how many parents don't really know how to be parents or how to keep house." In most instances she does some limited counseling, and then refers them to someone else. She has binders full of collaborative contacts for referrals...therapists who speak other languages...parenting classes for teen-age mothers... after school programs for children whose parents work...food banks...shelters...counselors for victims of abuse...the list goes on.

Loving children isn't enough, parents need to take care of them, protect them and provide for them.

What she and her co-workers do is emergency response. It is intervention, not really counseling, and not prevention. "We are called in to take care of immediate problems, and keep things from getting worse. I feel good about what we do and know that I have helped. But there needs to be more prevention programs, things like social workers in schools, parenting programs in the neighborhoods. It is difficult to get funding for programs like that because the results are not measurable—you never know what you prevent; while intervention programs can report how many people were served and what the problems were."

So the calls keep coming; from police, neighbors, even family members. "Some of the cases are sad and I get very touched, but I have learned to do what I can, and then leave it in the hands of God. My faith helps me accept what I can't do." One of her co-workers tells me "Martha is wonderful, she is so positive and genuine. She does more than take care of her cases, she takes care of us. We all look to her on bad days when we need cheering up. I don't know what this office would be like without her."

Dolls represent the battered, neglected, abused children which Sister Martha and her co-workers are trying to protect.

Walking Together

Sister Ann Marie Gelles
Elementary School Teacher • Reno, Nevada

A petite, athletic looking woman sat with twenty other adults in a meeting room, waiting nervously. She had looked forward to that day, but sitting there, she felt apprehensive. Then they called her name, "Sister Ann you will receive Nina, a female yellow lab." A half hour later, as she stroked the dense fur on Nina's neck, she knew this dog must become her new best friend. Together they went through four weeks of rigorous training at the Guide Dogs for the Blind. Nina was the second dog with whom she had gone through training, and Sister Ann wondered how she could ever love her and depend on her, like her first dog, Honey.

Blind since birth, Sister Ann Marie Gelles has learned she can do anything she wants, but having a guide dog makes it easier and gives her the independence on which she thrives. She remembers that day she got Nina, and how much they have come to depend on each other.

Sister Ann is a special education teacher at the elementary level for visually impaired children. Very few teachers of the blind are blind themselves, and getting to this position wasn't easy. In college, the Director of the Special Education Program told her she should not have enrolled, there was no way she was going to make it in elementary education. Then when it was time for student teaching, they said she would have to find her own position because they couldn't ask a teacher to supervise her, "it would be too much of a burden."

People only saw the blindness, not the person. They seemed happy to help the blind, to take care of them; but they had trouble believing a blind person could be the one who taught, who helped others, who served, which is what Sister Ann wanted to do. "All my life people have doubted what I could do, in response my motto has been 'I'll show them'." And she has. Disproving the naysayers, she rides horses, dances, lives alone, teaches and serves others.

When she first entered Sisters of the Holy Family, Sister Ann was a religious education teacher. She had felt called to be a sister, and called to teach, but still something was lacking. Finally she realized she belonged where her talents could be used more fully, working with children who were facing the same challenges she had faced. With the support of the SHF Leadership Team, she earned her credentials for teaching the visually impaired.

Teaching blind children is indeed her calling, carrying out the SHF mission to serve special children in a special way.

Currently, Sister Ann has four students in Nevada's Washoe County schools. Working closely with the parents, Sister Ann develops an individualized curriculum for each student. Typically she continues with students for several years; either sitting alongside them in the back of a regular classroom, working on the same lessons as the other children, while also teaching special skills like Braille and abacus; or outside the regular classroom in sessions devoted to developing special skills. For all of them, the goal is to be totally mainstreamed eventually.

Being a blind child is lonely, and frustrating...I can't take the pain away, I can only walk with them and maybe make the way a little easier.

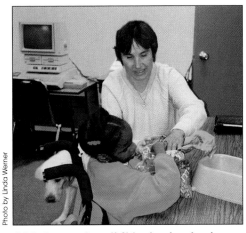

A blind person herself, Sister Ann teaches her students lessons that extend beyond the prescribed curriculum. Here she helps a student "learn by feeling" to feed a dog.

Not only does she teach them school curriculum, but she is an example for them, showing them how to live vibrantly as a blind person. "I have walked in their footsteps, I know what it is like... Being a blind child is lonely, and frustrating...I can't take the pain away, I can only walk with them and maybe make the way a little easier." Having been there herself, she also understands why blind children can become difficult, angry, and have behavior problems. She is always willing to forgive the hateful words and the tantrums that are part of the process, looking beyond them to the final goal.

Just as Sister Ann's goal is to make the way easier for her students, Nina makes the way easier for Sister Ann. Together they walk to school, to stores, to the health club. Being a guide dog takes incredible intelligence and constant attention, and Nina is on duty whenever they are away from home. Sister Ann acknowledges that twice her life has been saved by a guide dog pulling her out of the direct path of vehicles. But even the fright of those experiences does not deter her.

Sister Ann continues to open new doors as she expands her ministry, and serves a larger forum as an advocate for the blind. She has been a speaker at numerous functions, was featured on the Bay Area television program, *Mac and Motley,* and in the book *Guide Dog Puppy Grows Up.* In 1994, Sister Ann accomplished another first when she was asked to serve on the Board of Directors of Guide Dogs for the Blind, as their first blind member. "Being blind has enhanced my ministry and my ability to serve. I really feel God called me this way. I minister to the blind as a blind person."

Keeping Families Together

Sister Marie Deering
Crossroads Family Shelter • Las Vegas, Nevada

People come to Las Vegas for all different reasons, but many of them come for money. They soon find out that life is the same here as elsewhere, the grass isn't any greener, it isn't any easier to get a job or keep one, it still takes hard work to keep a family together, and after a few bad choices, entire families can find themselves homeless. It is at this point that they might find their way to the Crossroads Family Shelter. This is the only shelter in the county that provides for intact families, or single fathers with children. It is residential community living, not emergency shelter for one night. Getting admitted is not simply opening a door, there is usually a waiting list, and an interview with the staff is required. The families need to demonstrate that they are willing, and able, to live within the rules of the shelter before they will be admitted.

Dispensing tough love for families ...giving them a chance to get their lives in order.

Sister Marie Deering and the other staff members at Crossroads are dispensing tough love for families. Each family has a room of their own. There are communal bathrooms, laundry room, living room, and a minimal kitchen. Everything is provided for the family's basic needs; but this is not a free ride. Everyone is expected to do chores, both daily and weekly. Every family must have one member either looking for work, or working every day. They have to take care of their own children or arrange for child care. No drug or alcohol usage is permitted. If they get work, a percentage of their pay goes to the shelter. Sister Marie says "You have to be strong to work here. Some people have trouble with the rules, and I end up being a policer and a patroller, but it is the only way we can provide the kind of service we believe the families need. Our goal is to keep families together and to help them learn to take care of themselves."

In addition to shelter, food and clothing, the residents receive counseling. "Bad things happen to good people. People can end up homeless for many reasons beyond their control. Some need to honestly face their past in order to change their current circumstances. We try to provide whatever resources they need to get back on their feet...12 step programs... lessons in basic job skills and money managing...parenting classes." When they do get a job, Sister Marie encourages them to stay at the shelter for a little while, save their first few paychecks, and make sure they can take care of their family before they leave. The staff helps them find housing, and stays in contact with them for a year after they leave. "For some families this is the second chance they needed, or maybe the first chance they ever had to get their life in order and establish a home. When others leave we aren't at all sure they won't end up in the same situation again."

For 20 years Sister Marie Deering worked in the SHF Day Homes, always doing additional volunteer ministry in the evenings; Marriage Encounter, counseling for domestic violence, AIDS services; each a different expression of her mission to serve families. In 1990 she decided to devote herself entirely to working with adults. For one year she provided counseling and services to people suffering with AIDS. "It is very draining work, but so needed. I would have continued, but there was no funding, so I looked for someplace else that needed me." At Crossroads Family Shelter, she found a place to use many of the skills she had developed in her other ministries. "Being here is somewhat bittersweet. It isn't as cheerful as Day Home work, but I really feel what we are doing is important...Influencing adults is much harder than influencing children. With some families we succeed, with others we don't."

Sister Marie (on right) talks to Debbie, one of the residents, in the day room at the Crossroads Family Shelter. Debbie, who has been at the shelter for two weeks with her husband and two children, tells me, "I'm thankful for what the people here have done for us. I was pretty low when we got here, my husband is a painter, but he hadn't worked in a long time. We were living in the truck. Being here has made me start to feel hopeful again...and the atmosphere and structure, even all the rules, have been really good for my kids."

Nurturing Personal Growth

Sister Marietta Fahey
Educator, Counselor & Co-Director, Holy Family Center
Pleasant Hill, California

During the late 1960s when Sister Marietta Fahey was working in a parish she noticed that parishioners came to talk to her more about human issues than religious ones, and she saw a need for greater integration of spiritual life with personal life. So she began taking courses in human development and spirituality, received a Master's Degree in Applied Spirituality, and became a licensed PRH (Personnalité et Relations Humaines) educator.

Now she devotes her time to counseling, accompanying people in their growth, providing the kind of help she envisioned almost 25 years ago. She and her colleague, Sister Pat Kozak, CSJ, have a center in a quiet suburb in California where they provide workshops, retreats and individual counseling. Sister Marietta's work focuses on personal growth, and self-awareness. As she talks I can see why people feel comfortable talking to her. She is compassionate, insightful and wise, and she has a ready smile and a rippling laugh that puts you at ease.

"It is not possible
For people to rise,
To stand upright. . .
Without causing society to stir."
André Rochais
Founder of PRH

I met Sister Marietta at the Holy Family Center on a beautiful spring day. From the street the Center looked about the same size as the individual homes it sits between, but once inside I realized it is much larger. Immediately inside the front door is a large room, originally a chapel. Tall amber windows bathe the room with a warm glow, and create a peaceful, private setting for workshops and gatherings. Other rooms downstairs include individual counseling rooms, an office, kitchen, dining room and living room. Upstairs there are eight bedrooms, a sitting room and a prayer room. Nothing is fancy, but everything is warm, comfortable, restful. Every month there is at least one workshop extending over several days, during which the participants are invited to stay at the Center.

Sisters Pat and Marietta believe an important part of what they offer is the atmosphere and living at the Center. "We want people to experience a healthy, holistic style of living which includes time for oneself, enjoying simple things, good food and appreciating nature." They hope that the participants will take some of that lifestyle home with them, and begin to integrate it into their own lives.

The backyard is the highlight of the Center. Everyone gravitates to it. What an aggregation of plants! It is a casual place, no formal structure, just a collection of growing things that is constantly changing. The garden has several areas connected by walkways and stepping stones, so you walk around and among the vegetables and flowers. There are tables and chairs enough for scores of people to relax, read, eat and enjoy. The orange tree is full of fruit and we stop to pick some. This nurturing and life-affirming environment is a reflection of Sisters Marietta and Pat, and an extension of the gifts they offer clients.

Sisters Pat (left) and Marietta nurture both plants and people at the Holy Family Center.

Tune-ups for people

Sister Marietta tells me about the workshops she gives. "They are for anyone who wants to improve their personal life. We help them explore their identity, their purpose in life and their relationships. Many people that attend are in crisis or transition (divorce, problems with children) but one doesn't need to be in crisis to benefit from the workshops. Just like cars need tune-ups, so do people." The workshops are a starting point for personal exploration and growth. Afterwards, many continue by participating in monthly growth groups. Others prefer to continue through individual counseling.

Sister Marietta works mostly with adults. Women are usually the first ones in a family to seek outside help. "In our society, being introspective doesn't come as naturally to men as it does to women. Men are generally more concerned about projects, plans, external things. It is not uncommon for a woman to feel there is something wrong with a relationship, and the man to say 'We don't have a problem'." Frequently husbands come to counseling after they begin to see the difference it has made in their wives' lives. Much of Sister Marietta's work centers on fostering healthy relationships between people: couples, parents and children, co-workers.

Although Holy Family Center is owned by Sisters of the Holy Family, religion is not emphasized there because Sisters Marietta and Pat want everyone to feel welcome and comfortable, regardless of their religion. Many of their clients are Catholic, some are not practicing any religion, almost all of them are searching for something, either internally or externally. Sister Marietta's ministry is to these individuals and families...helping them find answers within themselves...unlocking their full potential...showing them how to be better partners and parents. The fruits of her ministry show in the changes in her clients' lives, and it is not uncommon for someone to seek her out after witnessing the results in a friend's life.

"The Sisters of the Holy Family devote their lives to visiting, relieving and consoling the poor, especially poor friendless families. They extend their charitable sympathy and aid night and day, to all who are in need."

Sister Dolores

On the Road

"Priests have often asked me what is the special work of Sisters of the Holy Family, and I have always said that they were gleaners—gleaners of souls. Priests can administer the Sacraments, but after all, there are many souls they can never reach." This was the vision shared by Father Prendergast with Lizzie Armer when they founded Sisters of the Holy Family. Their work was among the people, wherever they were. Instilled in every Sister during her novitiate days was Sister Dolores's credo: "You must be out of the house in the morning by 8:30, and among the people. We must always go to the people, they should not have to come to us."

The first thirty years, the Sisters worked in the neighborhoods of San Francisco. Then as word of their work spread among priests, they received requests to bring their unique kind of ministry to other parishes, and gradually they branched out geographically.

Enroute to a new Vacation School, these Sisters ponder if they've come the wrong way. Because driving was mostly a male activity in the early 1900s and many people were startled to see Sisters behind the wheel, Sisters of the Holy Family became known as "The Nuns Who Drive."

VACATION SCHOOLS

In 1929 the Sisters began a new kind of ministry, providing Vacation Schools in outlying communities that did not have regular religious education programs.

Walnut Creek, which was an hour and a half drive from their convent in Piedmont, was the site for one of the first Vacation Schools. The first day the Sisters arrived to find the church locked and no one around. After knocking on neighbors' doors, and resourceful negotiating, the Sisters were situated in a hall next door to the church, and a woman was sent out to broadcast their arrival. Eventually children began coming. By the end of the first day there were 21 students, and by the end of two weeks, they had taught 96 children, many coming from surrounding towns.

The Sisters loved the work, and the children loved the schools, telling the Sisters "it isn't like catechism at all." Based on the success of those first sessions in Walnut Creek and Concord, the next summer more pastors tried this new education program. Each year the numbers increased. In 1935, just six years since their first school, the Sisters from San Francisco had 3252 children registered in Vacation Schools, stretching from Eureka to Monterey to Reno.

Classes were held wherever they found space, under the trees or in garages.

Besides religious instruction, the Sisters always provided projects for the children in the afternoons.

WORKING OUTSIDE OF THE PARISH

Taking the Church to the People
Sisters helped prepare this Chapel Car and accompanied the priest on his visits from Fresno to outlying rural areas.

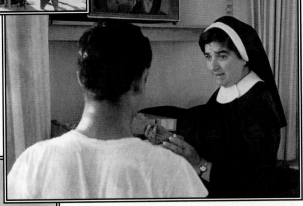

Chaplain in Prisons and Hospitals
Sister Dolores Molina gives a rosary to a man in an honor camp.

Home Visits
Because of Sister Eulalia McShane's many visits to this couple's home, the husband converted to Catholicism when he was 69.

Seeking People Out
The Sisters walked the neighborhoods to find children and families who were in need.

Providing the Warmth of Humanity

Sister Paulina Villa
Chaplain, West Bay Home Health Services • Daly City, California

"My daughter was four years old and having major emergency surgery. We were so scared. Then just when they were about to wheel her into the operating room, Sister Paulina appeared. She had made a special trip to San Francisco just to bless her and be with us. It meant so much to me that she did that." Janet Gore is the first of many to tell me how Sister Paulina Villa touched her life.

For one man, who lives in a second floor apartment, and has trouble carrying things since his surgery last year, Sister Paulina's visits are critical in his ability to continue to live alone. They never schedule a visit, she just stops by on Thursday afternoons to say hello. She knows he shops that day and she comes to carry his groceries upstairs for him. He would never ask for help, but as long as she is there visiting, it is OK.

As the chaplain at West Bay Home Health Services, Sister Paulina visits patients referred to her by doctors, nurses, therapists and friends. To the people she visits, she is someone who cares, who comes to see them because she is a friend. She provides emotional support, psycho-physical support and spiritual support.

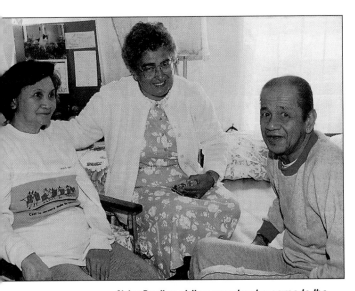

Sister Paulina visits a couple who came to the United States from the Philippines for the husband to have surgery. Recovery is taking longer than expected, and they are lonely being so far from home and family. Sister Paulina is one of the few people they know here.

"When we give up as nurses, we ask Paulina to step in. She always seems to know what people need most. I wouldn't want to run this place without her," says Barbra Headman, Director of West Bay, in her praise of Sister Paulina Villa. They worked together previously at Seton Medical Center, and Barbra had learned to rely on Sister Paulina. "She was much more than the chaplain...she added the warmth of humanity to everything we did. When I came to West Bay I felt like something was missing without Paulina, so at the first opportunity I asked her to join us here as our chaplain."

Together they created a unique position. Sister Paulina is the only home visiting chaplain on staff at a health care organization in the United States. In an average month she will make 120 home visits, bringing comfort, friendship and support to people up and down the San Francisco Peninsula. She is on call 24 hours a day, available whenever someone needs her, giving them emotional support before surgery, cheering them up when they are down, frequently being with people when they die. Unlike the rest of the staff of West Bay, Sister Paulina's services are not controlled by insurance rules, and Barbra puts no restrictions on who she visits, or how often. Her counseling includes family members as well as patients. Her services are a gift from the West Bay Board.

Paulina's friends say she has a sixth sense about who is most in need, and frequently changes her plans for a day because she feels someone needs her with them. Many times this intuition has brought her to the bedside of someone who is dying. She provides grief counseling to families, and continues to visit people even when they are no longer receiving services from West Bay. This freedom to provide totally for them, whoever they are, whatever they need, is what Sister Paulina likes best about her position at West Bay and is thankful to Barbra, "whose support and understanding of my ministry is what makes this position so unique."

The only home visiting chaplain on staff at a health care organization in the United States.

I accompany Paulina on a morning of visiting. The first stop is at Serra House, a Center for Independent Living where we are joined by Shaun Peterson, a SHF associate. We visit three women, all confined to wheelchairs, but totally unalike in their emotional and mental condition. Each receives a different form of caring from Shaun and Sister Paulina. Next we go to an apartment building in the Mission District of San Francisco. It is a very tiny apartment, but the people graciously make a place for us to sit, so happy to have visitors. Our last destination is an attractive middle class home in Daly City. Although totally different environments, the need for friendship and support is the same. To each person Sister Paulina offers a warm touch of her hand, a cheery smile and a caring heart.

Sister Paulina says "I have no agenda. I just meet people where they are and offer them friendship. If they are Catholic, I offer them Communion. If they need help, I find it for them. Each day is different...at any one time I am probably keeping track of a few hundred people."

During their visit to Serra House, Associate Shaun Peterson listens to Mellownee Molo tell about the great time she had yesterday with her daughter who Sister Paulina brought back into her life a year ago. "When Paulina was visiting one day, she asked about my family, I told her I hadn't seen my daughter in ten years. I guess Paulina found her, and called her...whatever she did, now my daughter comes to see me twice a week."

Loving the People

Sister Carolyn Whited
Pastoral Administrator, St. Thomas Aquinas • Wells, Nevada

In the rugged ranch country of northeastern Nevada, alongside Highway 80 on the outskirts of Wells, is a Catholic church. The Catholic community has been there for generations, but much of the time the nearest priest or sister has been 50 miles away in Elko. Now Sister Carolyn Whited is in residence, and the parish is being revitalized, and growing. Bringing people back to the Church has been her main task. "Almost everyone I met when I first came here said they were Catholic, but few were coming to church. Many of them didn't even know what it meant to be Catholic, they just said that because that's what they were as a child. They weren't married in the Church, had not been confirmed, and were not coming to Mass."

When I ask her how she is getting them back, she laughs and says "Anyway I can think of. Mostly by being available to people all the time, in lots of ways. Then if I see a glimmer of positive action, I lavish them with praise. I guess you could say, I love them back."

Re-introducing people to Church is often easiest by providing for children, so Sister Carolyn started an after school program for grades K-8, and six times a year has family events associated with the program, "to give them an easy entry to the Church." One family sent their children to the program and attended the family events consistently for two years. They had never been to Mass, and the children were not baptized. Then one Sunday, Sister Carolyn was thrilled to see the entire family walk in the church door. The children have now been baptized and they have all become regular attendees at Mass.

Every summer more than a third of the public school population attends elaborate ecumenical Vacation Bible Schools that Sister Carolyn coordinates. The parish hall is transformed to fit a theme like, "On Safari with Jesus" or "Sailing with Jesus," and enlisting the help of older teens, the lessons are told in skits and puppetry. In the center of it all is Sister Carolyn dispensing her love. Her presence energizes a room, children are spellbound with her storytelling.

Adults, too, are drawn to her. Sister Carolyn leans forward to tell me a story, "One Sunday at Mass I noticed a woman who was dressed in clothes a bit racier than what we normally see. She left before I had a chance to meet her, but a few weeks later she was back, and then again. Finally I got to meet her, and invited her to stop by the house and visit anytime. The next week she appeared at my door. When she said she lived across the street, I knew she meant the local house of prostitution." She needed someone to talk to, and sensed Sister Carolyn would be OK. "She told me about her life...'how she was a friend to lonely men.'

Sister Carolyn sees the common humanity, and nurtures the Godliness in each person.

Obviously she saw her life differently than I did! But I also heard a questioning in her voice and I resolved to help her change her life. I knew it would be a big hurdle for her, it wasn't going to happen right away, but we had to make it happen.

We've had many talks since then. She admits she wants to change, but is afraid, it is the only life she has ever known. The other women are her friends and her security. She even persuaded me to come over to their house one day because she said, 'I've been telling the others about you, and I think some of them would like to talk to you, but are afraid to come over here.'" Sister Carolyn raises her eyebrows and laughs when she says, "I never thought I'd go to a house of prostitution, but I did, I couldn't say no to this chance to reach out to people."

Listening to her talk, I understand why people confide in her. She loves them. Her counseling can be a delicate balance of accepting and loving the person, but clearly disapproving of their actions. She takes this same attitude to the Honor Camp where she ministers to the inmates every week. "Many of the men have really opened up, I have become part pastor and part mother for them...I feel God's presence more strongly when I'm there than any other time." Sister Carolyn sees the common humanity, and nurtures the Godliness in each person.

This inclusive spirit is the gift that Sister Carolyn has brought to St. Thomas Aquinas, where everyone is made to feel welcome. She inspired the establishment of a new branch of the Knights of Columbus, the first organization in town to bring men of different social strata together on an equal footing. She seeks out both the ranch owners and the laborers. "My door is always open to anyone. We don't work by appointment here, so I might be doing bookkeeping or writing the newsletter, but when someone comes to the house, I just put it aside. The people come first, the paperwork will always be there."

Now every Sunday the church is full. Many people drive from sixty miles away to attend, and come only sporadically, but gradually they are coming back. Parish participation is

Surrounded by people, laughing and talking, is where Sister Carolyn can most often be found.

growing; still, both the diocese and Sisters of the Holy Family must continue to provide subsidies. Recently when there was talk of losing their subsidy, which would mean losing Sister Carolyn, one ranching family told her they would take out a loan if necessary to keep her in Wells. They know how important her presence has been for everyone.

As I get up to leave, Sister Carolyn gives me a big bear hug, and I feel the love her parishioners don't want to lose, the encompassing love she offers everyone she meets.

A Bridge Between

Sister Ancila DeLaO
Hispanic Ministries, St Mary's of Assumption • Park City, Utah

This really is carrying out our charism to be gleaners. There are times I feel I am picking one grain at a time.

Sister Ancila DeLaO knew since second grade that she wanted to be a sister. She grew up in New Mexico, but everyone she knew was Hispanic, and their culture was more Mexican than American. Her mother was aghast at the idea of Ancila entering religious life, as she had planned that Ancila would care for them in their old age. It took 29 years of convincing before her parents consented for her to leave home to join Sisters of the Holy Family. That was her first calling. Her second calling came one summer, several years later, when she went with Sister Elaine Marie Sanchez to Tijuana. They did basic pastoral work and lived with the people in their homes. "The people I met there were like sheep without a shepherd. They had so little, but their faith and desire were so strong. I knew then that my life's work was to serve the Hispanic community."

For seven years, 1985–1992, the SHF Mission Fund sponsored Sister Ancila as a missionary in Mexico. The first three years she was with Sister Victor Negrete, then four years by herself. Working with the people, they physically and spiritually built four colonias (which are small neighborhood chapels and the communities that they serve). The presiding pastor had 11 chapels to serve, spread out over a large area, so the Sisters were the daily real presence of the Church for the people. Sister Ancila conducted services from youth ministry to burials.

Then in 1993, another member of Sisters of the Holy Family, Sister Karen Stern, who was working at St. Mary's in Park City, Utah, had a problem that she thought Sister Ancila could solve. Sister Karen and the pastor wondered why there were so few Hispanics at church when there were so many in the area, so they asked Sister Ancila to come for a week and do a survey of the needs of Hispanics in the area. "They sent me a round trip ticket, so I knew I only had one week. I went to the streets, highways, hotels and housing developments to interview people. I did 78 interviews that week. Overwhelmingly what I heard was that their greatest need was to learn English." After reviewing her report, the parish created a new position and asked Sister Ancila to return to serve the Hispanic community in an outreach position.

While Park City may be a fabulous resort to skiers and a gold mine to real estate developers, to many of the people who labor at the resorts, it is a city with expensive housing, little day care, and poor wages. At the winter resorts, the kitchens and housekeeping departments are filled with people who each work two and three jobs, at minimum wage, to try to earn enough money to last through several months of summer unemployment. Sister Ancila says,

Sister Ancila DeLaO ministers to the Hispanic parishioners at St Mary's of the Assumption. Pastor Robert Bussen explains how important her work is in his parish, "While in other locales throughout the country countless numbers of Hispanics are turning to evangelical groups to meet their personal needs, here in Park City they rest secure among us, since Sister Ancila is the undisputed pastoral presence who meets their needs."

"Their shoulders and hands are needed, but the persons are not acknowledged." It is her mission to change that. She is a bridge between the Hispanic community and the rest of the city. She has become a well known spokesperson, and local media often seek her out. She was recently given a scholarship by the city to participate in the Park City Leadership 2000 Program.

Advocacy work is only part of what Sister Ancila does, she also works hands-on to meet the needs of her community. She organized and teaches an "English as a Second Language" program, getting the city to donate the space and enlisting other people to help with the teaching. Two days a weeks she joins Sister Angela Marie Hinckley at the St. Lawrence Mission Thrift Shop, which has become a center for help to the poor. Every week, Sister Ancila can be found there, reading and interpreting papers and documents for Hispanics who have not yet mastered English.

Her compelling mission is to empower her people, to build their self-esteem, to teach them what they need in order to help themselves. It is a long term effort, and progress is not fast. Slowly the Hispanics are being integrated into the parish. About her work, Sister Ancila says, "This really is carrying out our charism to be gleaners. There are times I feel I am picking one grain at a time."

A Place of Their Own

Sister Gladys Guenther
Pastoral Administrator, Our Lady of Guadalupe • Lathrop, California

A dozen pre-teens are gathered in a garage on a Friday evening. Most of them have been coming here three nights a week all summer long. Sister Gladys's house has become their place, which is exactly what she hoped for when she persuaded the Diocese of Stockton to buy the house last spring. As the Pastoral Administrator in Lathrop she realized there was no safe place in town for the youths to hang out, not even a place they could meet to have a soft drink, and talk like they need to do. She wanted to give them a place of their own.

Sister Gladys Guenther has been working with youths for many years, and for the past two summers has been specifically involved in gang prevention ministry. "The pre-teen years are a crucial time in determining what direction kids will go," Sister Gladys explained. "They are asserting themselves as independent people from their parents and family. No matter what their parents are like, the kids want to be apart from them. As much as they are fighting to be separate from the family, they are not usually strong individuals yet. They need to be part of a group. That is why they are most susceptible to gangs at this age. Gangs offer them an identity, an automatic acceptance by a group, and a chance to prove they are independent."

Painting this mural has given the youths a project of their own, something they will be able to point to with pride for all the town to see. While they paint, they just hang out together and talk, with a little supervision from Sister Gladys.

There are always snacks at Sister Gladys's. These girls serve cookies they made this afternoon. Their own combinations of cereals, chocolate bits, peanut butter, marshmallows--the cookies are unbeliev- ably sweet to my taste, but they love them! Sister Gladys, a creative cook herself, is always willing to let anyone help, or experiment in the kitchen.

Her solution is to give them those same things: self-esteem, a peer group, and independence, in a safe environment. In their laid-back way, the kids told me the program is working, "Yea, Sister Gladys is cool." "On Tuesdays and Thursdays we usually talk about stuff...like why it is stupid to join gangs...why we should stay in school...but Sister Gladys doesn't lecture us." "I like to just hang out here, 'cause she's OK."

Tuesday and Thursday evenings in the summertime they have Discussion Group, Friday evening is for activities. Afternoons and other evenings, kids frequently stop by. Sister Gladys encourages them to plan the activities they want, and she will help make it happen. When they wanted to go camping, she assembled donations of food from local food processing plants and planned the menus around what she received. When they wanted to go skating for a day, she helped them find ways to earn money to pay for the day's outing. Currently she is looking for a ballroom dancing teacher, to prepare them for dancing the traditional waltz at Quinceañeras.

Tonight they are working on a mural they have been painting for several months. The six plywood panels, each four feet by eight feet, depicting the story of Our Lady of Guadalupe, will be displayed during Las Posadas on the empty lot, which is the future site of their church. The youths are looking forward to having the whole town see their artwork.

Sister Gladys's house has also become a center for other activities. Tonight while the youths paint in the garage, the choir practices in the living room, and afterwards there will be a birthday party for one of the members. A few times a month, evening prayer meetings are held here. Sister Gladys has indeed brought the church to the neighborhood.

Grassroots Ministry

Sister Carol Reichert
Pastoral Associate • Burkesville and Albany, Kentucky

Traveling a hilly rural road, the countryside green with lush undergrowth and saplings crowding each other in their race for the sky, Sister Carol Reichert admires the scenery around her and thanks God again for bringing her here. Several times a week she travels this route between the two parishes she serves in southern Kentucky, Holy Cross in Burkesville and Emmanuel in Albany. They are both mission parishes with a total of only 45 families, but Sister Carol is much busier than she expected to be when she accepted the position here.

Ministering with human kindness and friendliness.

Her mission is not just to serve Catholics, but to be active and visible in the community. Catholics are a tiny minority in Kentucky, less than one percent of the population, and historically there has been prejudice against them. So for both Sister Carol and Pastor Larry Gelthaus part of their job is to continue to break down the prejudice and gain acceptance. Being involved with other clergy in the ministerial association, rotating with others as chaplain at the local hospital and nursing home, and serving on the board of Habitat for Humanity, has brought Sister Carol into the lives of many people who never knew a Catholic before. "The other clergy have been wonderful to work with. We have developed many ecumenical activities: joint outreach programs, combined worship services, and recently we exchanged pulpits for a day. We have seen how much we have in common."

The other part of her work is grassroots, personal, one-on-one service; and there is no lack of opportunity for this ministry. This is a very poor area, more than a third of the people are below the poverty level. Many of them are on welfare, and have been for generations. There are few jobs available, and expectations are low. People are hidden away in remote areas, frequently living in deteriorating homes. Many of them are elderly and lonely. As Sister Carol visits them and gets acquainted, she makes note of their individual needs. Then several times a year, she organizes high school and college students to repair, clean or fix some of these homes as part of the Appalachian Service Project. The students, who arrive for two to five days of volunteer work, mostly from affluent cities on the East Coast, find this is an eye-opening experience. They patch roofs, build steps, clean houses, level paths and, equally appreciated by many of the elderly, the students visit with them.

Human kindness and friendliness have a high value here. The pace of life is totally different than in the San Francisco Bay Area Sister Carol left two years ago. "The frantic life of the big cities was getting to me. The natural setting I found here feeds my spirit. I see so many ways I can help...This area has always been a male dominated society, the women have very low self-worth, so my next effort will be to find a way to work with women in building their self-esteem." Sister Carol's blend of contemporary womanhood and traditional caring are the right tools for nurturing personal growth in people unaccustomed to change.

A Weekend of
Volunteer Work

As part of the Appalachian Service Project, Sister Carol Reichert and students from Holy Cross College in Worcester, Massachusetts, spent a day cleaning homes, doing minor repairs and visiting with residents in rural Burkesville.

The next day was spent renovating a building to house the new Cumberland County Food Pantry.

"It would be the joy of my life to see the Sisters of the Holy Family in every district not only of this city, but in outside parishes where there are no parochial schools...Your work goes farther than the work of the schools, for they cannot reach all."

Father John Prendergast

Teachers Outside of Schools

Parochial schools have long been a tradition in the Catholic Church, yet there have always been more children in public schools than in parochial schools. It was for the public school children of San Francisco that Sisters of the Holy Family began providing religious education, first at Cathedral Parish, then at St. Francis Parish.

At St. Francis, the boys were considered quite unmanageable and it had become the custom of the pastor to lock the doors during classes so the boys would not escape. On the first Sunday that Sisters of the Holy Family came to St. Francis, Sister Joseph was assigned to teach the boys, and given lots of warning about the bad behavior she could expect. With some trepidation, she decided to appeal to their honor, and began class by announcing the doors were open, no one need leave by way of the windows, and anyone was free to leave before the lessons commenced. Perhaps caught by surprise, everyone stayed, and Sister Joseph proceeded to keep them there by making the class interesting and enjoyable, a technique that has remained at the heart of all instruction by Sisters of the Holy Family.

Classes became quite large at most of their parishes. The Sisters were constantly inviting children in the neighborhoods, and the children themselves would bring friends to learn from these friendly Sisters. Above are Sunday School pupils from St. Peter and St. Paul in San Francisco during a Columbus Day celebration.

The Sisters were soon in demand wherever new parishes were established, which led them to establish convents in many other cities.

They taught every day of the week in order to cover the many districts to which they had been assigned. At one count, they were teaching religious education to 10,000 children a year.

They developed their own system for teaching religious education, designed to integrate theory with application and stories. Teachers used charts, books and pictures to capture the children's attention.

Experts at staging tableaus and special events, the Sisters' May Day processions, Christmas pageants and Fatima Days have been enjoyed by thousands of children and their parents.

"If it were not for Sisters of the Holy Family, there would be no Catholicism in California."

Don Boyd

In 1921, Sisters of the Holy Family first moved beyond the San Francisco Bay Area when they established a house in Los Angeles, soon they had Sisters in many California cities, and eventually in the other Western States.

In California
Sisters of the Holy Family
taught in all corners of the state:
from Eureka to Chula Vista
from Monterey to Placerville
from Santa Clarita to Eagle Rock.

Beyond California
the Sisters brought
religious education to children in:
Nevada • Washington
Hawaii • Alaska • Texas
Utah • Kentucky • South Dakota
Mexico

Frequently only two Sisters would be assigned to parishes with hundreds of children, so they recruited lay people to help them. SHF was one of the first religious orders to empower the laity within the Church, teaching them to be catechists, just as they taught their own Sisters during their formation.

Teaching expanded to include programs for all ages. They offered spiritual guidance through Retreats, Bible Study and Young Ladies' Institutes.

Respected as excellent catechists, for decades Holy Family Sisters have been selected as diocesan leaders of religious education programs. Sister Celestine Delehanty wrote a series of popular catechism books in the 1930s which were given to young children for many years. During the 1950s two members of Sisters of the Holy Family, Sister Leonard Donovan and Sister Esther Bazzano, helped Sister Maria de la Cruz Aymes, HHS, develop a new series of graded catechism books, incorporating some of the teaching methods the Holy Family had been using. The resulting "On Our Way Series" formed the spirituality of a generation of young Catholics, and was a valuable model for the continuing renewal of religious material for children.

Master Catechist

Sister Joan Marie Derry
Director of Adult Formation/Evangelization, San Rafael Parish
Rancho Bernardo, California

Having finished preparing a banquet for dozens of people, the chef went to the dining room to see if everyone was happy. A man was giving a talk, and it caught the chef's interest, so he stayed to listen. This was a dinner for Sister Joan Derry's adult religious education board from San Rafael Parish. All the lay leaders of the parish were there, telling about their individual ministries, and how the spirit was infusing the community. It was impressive to see the broad scope of what was going on in their parish, how many different programs they had, how deeply committed the lay people were. A spirit of camaraderie, joy and giving filled the room, and enveloped the chef. He went to Sister Joan and told her that he had been away from the Church for many years, but he was so moved by what he heard tonight, by the love of the people, that he would like to talk about recommitting to his Catholic faith.

As an RCIA (Rite of Christian Initiation for Adults) catechist, this was far from a new experience for Sister Joan; yet, the moment was still profound to her. To see the kindling of faith is the joy of evangelization. "It isn't always easy for people to come to faith, especially for adults who have been away from the Church, or never felt part of it. Acknowledging faith can be a struggle. Pressure from outside against their decision can be very strong." Part of the role of an RCIA catechist is to be prepared to help people through this struggle in their journey.

RCIA is only one form of adult religious education that is Sister Joan's responsibility at San Rafael Parish. She also has classes in Marriage and Family Enrichment, teaches catechists and prepares Bible Study leaders. She is a masterful teacher, and has devoted most of her life to religious education, working for years at the diocesan offices of Oakland and the Archdiocese of San Francisco.

Contributed photo. Photographer unknown.

Sister Joan Derry leads a Bible Study group at San Rafael

From the late 1800s to the mid 1900s, hundreds of thousands of children received religious education from Sisters of the Holy Family and other catechetical communities. In some dioceses, lay people were also trained as catechists. Some teachers had degrees in theology, some had training as teachers, others were trained through practical experience. Each diocese had its own system of education. In 1970, while working at the Archdiocese of San Francisco, Sister Joan Derry was given the task to bring uniformity to the training of catechists throughout the Archdiocese.

Sister Joan developed a course of study for Master Catechists, the teachers of teachers. The Master Catechist program includes courses in theology, developmental psychology and education. Sister Joan said, "Theology alone isn't enough to be a good teacher of religious education, we needed to integrate specific skills for teaching religion and faith formation." Both vowed religious and laity throughout California are now trained in similar programs under guidelines which were adopted by the California Bishops' Conference in 1980.

Having so successfully implemented the Master Catechist program, Sister Joan was next asked to be the Associate Director of the new Permanent Diaconate program, a program restored with Vatican II, which gives both married and single men an opportunity to be ordained in the Church. Her role was to design academic and spiritual formation programs for deacons who would serve the Church in outreach ministry. In California, the first group of 35 men were ordained in 1975 after completing three years of study. Although they have authority to preach, baptize and marry, most of them are working in areas such as family counseling, youth services, prisons and outreach programs to poor and needy—very similar to the ministry of Sisters of the Holy Family.

Sister Joan is now back in a parish, but there is one more program she would like to see adopted throughout the state: a unified and comprehensive preparation for RCIA Master Catechists. At her parish, she already requires teachers of adults to have as much training as the teachers of children, and has developed a specific program for them. That is not yet true throughout California. "What happened that night in the restaurant was a result of the faith formation of the laity, we need to make sure we provide them the foundation so their faith can grow, and they can be strong Christian witnesses."

Formation of
the Heart

Sister Mercedes Braga
Ministry of Faith Formation, Holy Trinity • El Dorado Hills, California

Christianity is two thousand years old, and the core beliefs of Catholicism have been constant throughout history. However, like all vital organizations, the Church is not static, it continually evolves, develops, modifies. Today, leading a new direction in religious education are Sister Mercedes Braga, SHF and Sister Esther O'Mara, IBVM. They call it Catholic Family Formation. It is a big departure from how religious education has been taught in the American Catholic Church for the past century.

Family Formation makes faith formation in children, which has historically been viewed as the responsibility of priests and sisters, the responsibility of parents. Sister Mercedes explains the basis for this new program, "In my 40 years of teaching religious education, it became apparent that families need to be involved if faith is going to take hold. Parents can't just send children to catechism class for a couple of years and expect they will become true believers. This program was developed because it is our goal to provide more than education, we are trying to give them 'formation of the heart'."

Sister Mercedes teaches families how to nurture their own faith, giving them lesson plans to be taught weekly in the home. The lessons are designed to be enriching both for children and parents. Families are encouraged to be flexible about how they integrate the lessons with their lives, doing it whatever day and time works for them. In addition, the parents have preparation for each lesson, and the children have homework. When the concept was first introduced, there was apprehension and resistance from parents who typically said "I can't teach my children about religion, I don't know enough. That's what you are for."

Photo by Dennis Studer

George Vogt, Theresa Rozowski and their children, like each family who chooses to participate in Family Faith Formation, are given the program materials and personal introductory instruction by Sister Mercedes.

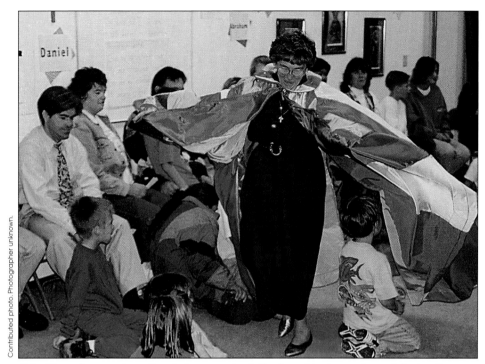

Sister Mercedes, wearing a "coat of many colors", like Joseph's, dances to music before the Scripture Stories are told. Theatrical embellishments and activities are trademarks of Sister Mercedes and part of what makes the family sessions so popular, and endears her to children.

Those parents have found that they knew more than they thought and that they are continuing to learn with their children. Five times a year all the families come together for a theme program, led by Sisters Mercedes and Esther. These programs usually include one of Sister Mercedes' famous skits, inspirational training and a chance to share with other families. The rest of the year, the staff is available to help the parents and show them how to proceed. "We are guides, we provide the materials, but they have to do it. We are teaching them how to read scripture and how to use it."

Almost 200 families with over 400 children are enrolled in this new kind of religious education at Holy Trinity. Response has been enthusiastic. Talking about religion and faith within the family is more intimate, and involves each person in a way that going to a class does not. Parents are expanding their knowledge about religion and are pleased to be sharing it with their children. Both parents and children enjoy the weekly sessions, which are sometimes their only time of truly personal sharing in hectic lifestyles.

Carrying on the Holy Family tradition of leadership in religious education, Sister Mercedes is now taking this program to other parishes and training their staff to facilitate Family Formation.

"How admirable a thing it would be to devote one's whole life to others, to live for them, to work for them, to die in their service."

Mother Dolores

Serving Special People

When the earthquake hit San Francisco in 1906, the horror of the devastation was more than some people could face, and they lost their reason. With no treatment available, except rest and time, Sisters of the Holy Family converted their still standing convent into a refuge for these distraught people; an expression of their devotion to help those most in need.

In the 1950s Sister Miriam Auxilium O'Gara found another expression of this devotion when she began working with the developmentally disabled. These were children and adults that others dismissed as not able to learn, but Sister Miriam believed they could understand religion, if it was presented to them in their terms; for religion is not based on learning as much as on the relationship of love, and she knew they could feel and give love with all their hearts. She brought religion to the developmentally disabled and they embraced it with ardor.

Eventually, what began as a ministry to provide for the spiritual needs of this special group of people, whom Sister Miriam called her "Holy Innocents," became a ministry to provide for their physical needs as well. Sister Miriam established residential homes for them which are still in operation in San Francisco.

Sister Miriam and a group of her "Holy Innocents" on the day of their First Communion.

Advent wreaths, sold in parishes throughout the city, were made by Sister Josephine Crowley and other Helpers of the Holy Innocents. The wreaths not only brought in needed funds, they brought public attention to the developmentaly disabled, and resurrected the use of advent wreaths in Catholic homes as a means of family worship.

Sister Marian McNamee with one of her Special Olympians.

Rose Kennedy honored Sister Miriam in 1968 for her work with the mentally and physically challenged.

Sisters Marian McNamee and John Minetta continued the work begun by Sister Miriam. Sister Marian established the New Vista Ranch in Nevada, and Sister John went to New Jersey to establish a national office for religious education for the developmentally disabled. Many other Sisters served other groups with special needs.

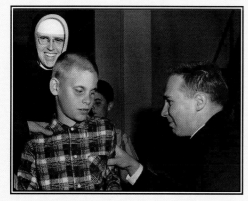

Sister Margaret Mary Nelligan at the School for the Blind in Berkeley.

Sister John Minetta with a group of her students.

With Pure Hearts

Sister Aurora Pérez
Director of SPRED (Special Religious Education of the Developmentally Disabled)
Oakland, California

With arms arching high in the air, six men and women stand in the front of the room swaying to the music, heads lifted in adoration. The hundreds of people seated in front of them imitate their actions in miniature. Singing "Pour out your love on your servant," they sweep their arms across their bodies and the movement spreads across the room like ripples of love on the sea of people.

This is a Mass for the developmentally disabled. Each song, reading and even the homily is accompanied by liturgical movement. In simple gestures...a gentle hand on a shoulder, radiant faces turned upward, slow pirouettes and gliding steps...small groups of developmentally disabled members of SPRED portray the essence of the message as the priest talks or the choir sings. It is one of the most spiritual services I have ever experienced. Love is flowing, not just from the pulpit outward, but from all the people in the room. They are participating with all their bodies and minds and hearts. They are truly worshiping with each other.

Sister Aurora Pérez is the reason this service happens. She planned it, scripted it, selected the music, and coached the priest. She is the Director of SPRED, and the heart and soul of this ministry to a population of friends with very special needs. Before SPRED, the developmentally disabled were not served by most parishes because they didn't know how to reach them. SPRED and Sister Aurora do.

SPRED uses Montessori techniques to teach religious education, centering each lesson around objects of everyday life to communicate religious ideas and feelings. They teach the same concepts as the rest of the Church, just in a different way. "One-on-one communication and individual participation is what makes our program so effective," says Sister Aurora. "The developmentally disabled don't learn by watching someone else, only by their own experience, so we design everything to engage the participation of each person. Music and liturgical movement are important ways of allowing the participants to express emotions they feel, but have trouble vocalizing."

Watching Sister Aurora mingle with everyone, it is apparent she has a special gift, an intuitive way of working with her friends, knowing how to reach them on a different level. After the service many come to hug her, to make sure she knows they are there. Few words are spoken, but much is communicated by the look in their eyes. They are grateful for what she has given them, which is much more than just religious education. SPRED is a life enriching program. It helps the participants see themselves in a more positive way, giving them self-esteem, teaching them to love themselves as they learn to love God. In SPRED they have found more than religion, they have found a social life, and friends.

In 1977 when the Oakland Diocese hired Sister Aurora to develop SPRED, no one had any idea how large this program would become. Today they have over 400 participants at the eighteen SPRED centers in the diocese. The lay people that Sister Aurora recruits and trains as catechists from each parish are the core of the program. They are individually paired with students, and stay with them for several years. The volunteers do not see themselves as teachers as much as friends...going on a faith journey...learning, sharing, and receiving as much as giving.

The connection between Sister Aurora and her students is almost magical. They are drawn to her as a kindred spirit.

The smile on Gina's face conveys how proud and happy she is to be a part of this service. When she joined SPRED 12 years ago she couldn't look at people or meet them. She was totally uncomfortable around strangers. Today she is performing in front of hundreds of them, full of self-esteem and joy.

Mostly They Listen

Sister Jacinta Fiebig
Center for AIDS Services • Oakland, California

I am on my way to meet Sister Jacinta who works at the Center for AIDS Services in Oakland, and I am a little apprehensive, I have prepared myself to see sadness and sick people. I come in the back door so I can get a sense of the place while I am alone, and become comfortable with it.

Surprise! What a cheerful place...children playing, people chatting. Beautiful bright banners hang from the ceiling, decorating a warm, modern setting. On this cold, rainy winter day the fireplace in the lounge is the center of activity. People sit on the hearth and the sofas visiting. The atmosphere is rather like a union at a small college with a rich blend of races and cultures and ages.

An attractive, petite woman with soft white hair is walking briskly towards me. I've been discovered, this is Sister Jacinta. Before she reaches me, someone spies her and rushes up to give her a big hug. The first of many hugs I'll see today.

In the 1980s AIDS came into the conscience of the American public and into the life of Sister Jacinta, a pastoral minister in South Dakota. One evening watching a news broadcast about people with AIDS, she knew that somehow this was the ministry where she belonged, these were people who needed her. She just had to find the specific place. In 1988, she arrived at the Center for AIDS Services in Oakland. Her parishioners at Our Lady of Perpetual Help Cathedral in Rapid City, South Dakota and the Mission Fund of Sisters of the Holy Family had pledged to support her as she worked as a volunteer at the Center for six months. She has never left. Six months stretched into two years as a volunteer, then she became one of the salaried staff, eventually the Pastoral Care Director, and the heart of the center. This indeed is where she belongs.

She and her staff of five volunteers provide emotional and spiritual support for the 900 clients of the Center. Mostly they listen. "Giving pastoral care doesn't mean wanting to change people, it just means being here for them when they need us, and listening. We need to walk where they are walking. Experience their pain. Share their triumphs."

Although the Center serves people from many walks of life, the majority of the clients are poor, many live on the streets. For them the Center is a refuge, and many come every day.

At the Center they can shower, eat, do their laundry, and be with other people. There is counseling, therapeutic massage and acupuncture. It is not a health care facility. It is a day center, a meeting place, a place where they are accepted. "The most important thing we offer is love. We strive to love every person who comes to us unconditionally and non-judgementally," Sister Jacinta says. "The common pain unites us as a community. The staff and clients are together learning to deal with this pain."

> *"Whatever you think, whatever you say, Sister Jacinta always understands."*

Ron, one of the clients tells me, "Whatever you think, whatever you say, Sister Jacinta always understands. She is the only one that is still here from the early days. She won't leave us or disappear. Her message is always 'Welcome—don't be afraid, this is a place of God.'" The message is conveyed as much by gesture, manner and action as by words. Sister Jacinta never talks about God or religion to the clients until they bring it up. She doesn't preach, she guides, letting them lead the conversation. They talk about their lives, emotions and fears, exploring their spirituality and emotional health.

Although the Center was founded by a Catholic brother, it is non-denominational and welcomes people of any faith, providing religious services from several denominations. The pastoral care extends beyond the Center into home visits and hospital visits as patients become weaker and sicker. Sister Jacinta is often called by hospitals who have found her card in a dying patient's belongings. Over 500 of her clients have now died from AIDS, and there is no end in sight. Every one of them steals a little piece of her heart, but they also give her the strength to keep giving.

While we have been sitting and talking in Sister Jacinta's little office, various people have stopped in to say hi, or wave as they pass by. Now Larry and his 20 month old daughter, Porsche, come in to visit. Larry has been coming here for a year. He is a tall, good looking black man, seemingly healthy, but "living with AIDS". He tells me the statistics of his blood count, the numbers come too fast for me to grasp—I don't know the lingo, but it doesn't matter, I know from the tone of his voice he is saying, "So far, so good."

Sister Jacinta leaves to take care of someone, and Larry tells me his story:

> *"When I see her, I see the spirit of God."*

He was a drug addict. Then one day, a little over a year ago, he decided he wanted to change his life. His new daughter, Porsche, was a big reason for that. He has been clean ever since. The Center and Sister Jacinta are a main reason he has been able to do that.

"I have never met anyone like Sister Jacinta before, you can just feel that she cares. If she could trade places with me, I know she would. When I see her I see the spirit of God. I can talk to her about anything with 100 percent trust. She taught me to love myself...and she helped me bring God into my life. My

life is immensely better. I am not Catholic but I get a lot of comfort from attending Sister's Mass on Tuesdays. This Center is a spiritual base for me."

All the while Larry talks, he plays little games with his daughter. I have trouble imagining this articulate man, this caring father, as a drug addict. What a long way he has come in a year. Now, with Sister Jacinta's help he is working towards bringing his other children back home from the foster care they were placed in when he was on drugs.

Re-connecting people with their families is a large part of Sister Jacinta's ministry. Many clients have drifted away from family because they have different values and lifestyles. But there is still a relationship. "They want to be reunited with their family…and many times they would love to go back home to die, but don't feel that's possible." She counsels them to make the effort, to not leave things unfinished. "One of the saddest things I see is family members who show up after a loved one has died of AIDS and there's been no closure."

Most people come to the Center long before their final illness or death. They come when they are "living with AIDS" and looking at life and death in a new way. To be with them through their journey is Sister Jacinta's role. "I have learned so much from these people. It has been like hearing the gospel all over again…it has given me a new view of the vow of poverty— to understand my own poverty of ability, to recognize how much there is that I can't affect…I wouldn't trade all the rest of my life for these six years." And the clients wouldn't trade her for anything. Ron speaks for many of them saying, "In the Bible they talk about angels; all I can tell you is that Sister Jacinta is one of them."

For Children Who Face Death

Sister Barbara McCall
Chaplain and Children's Grief Support • San Francisco Area, California

A woman with four jobs, Sister Barbara McCall rattles off her titles in a breathless voice. She has so much she wants to tell me, it is hard to know where to begin. The titles are immaterial, what she does is provide counseling and caring to the sick, especially to critically ill children, and children whose parents are critically ill.

She works with children both individually and in groups, frequently centering her counseling around play because young children can act out how they feel, better than they can talk about it.

Many of the children she sees have cancer and have been in and out of radiation, chemotherapy and surgery. They are remarkably resilient and brave, but need someone to help them deal with their emotions and understand what is happening inside and around them. They need someone to talk to outside of their family.

At Kaiser Hospice in Walnut Creek, California, Sister Barbara meets weekly with children who are dealing with the impending death of a family member. These children often need support even more than children who are ill themselves. They irrationally blame themselves for their parent's illness, and worry about what will happen to them if their parent dies. When a sibling is sick, the well child often feels guilty for being well, and lonely as their parent's attention is focused on the ill child. They take on the burdens and responsibilities of adults, and hide their feelings behind falsely brave faces.

In Sister Barbara, these children find someone who understands, someone they can talk to, someone who has time just for them. She can not change the circumstances, but she can help them sort through their emotions. She can help them find ways to cope with fear and anger. She offers them reassurance that they are not alone.

Sister Barbara has invited me to join her at the Robert Louie Family Cancer Support Group. This is a non-profit group founded by the family and doctor of a child who died of cancer.

Because they knew that when a child has cancer it affects the whole family, they established this group to give support to everyone—the parents, the child, the siblings. Meeting in a group of classrooms at Temple Emanu-el in San Francisco are 12 parents, 11 children and three facilitators. After a quick meal and a little visiting, the parents go into one room and the children come across the hall with Sister Barbara and her co-facilitator, Robin Kramer.

Old beyond their years ...their childhood innocence has been tempered by the realities of cancer.

The evening is very casual, most everyone sits or lounges on the floor. Sister Barbara has them introduce themselves, and tell about their illness. The children talk about it very matter-of-fact, no tears, no emotion. They say "I have leukemia" the same way they would say "I have brown eyes." (The parents, across the hall, are the ones who choke on their words, and go through boxes of tissues as they talk.) Sister Barbara asks, "Has anyone ever been mean to you?" Everyone wants to talk, the kids have lots to say. They definitely recognize mean behavior. They have a clear vision of right and wrong, not muddied by years of compromises. They talk about how it hurts when people are mean. Most of them have stories of being made fun of because they are sick.

Kelsey, who is in the process of losing her hair due to radiation, says some kids have been pulling out her hair when they sit behind her at school. "But,"

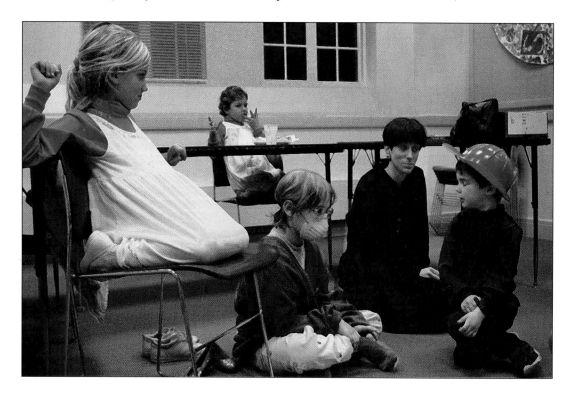

she says, "I don't care, it doesn't hurt like it would have before. I really can't feel it you know. And they don't mean to be mean, they just don't know how to be nice...sometimes people do bad things because they aren't happy inside. I just try to be nice to them so they can be happier." This little girl, who has plenty of reason to feel sorry for herself, has risen above those petty feelings, and is teaching others about charity.

Sister Barbara and Robin lead the discussion in such a gentle way. Little questions, lots of understanding nods. Sister Barbara's years of day home work are apparent in her mannerisms and big expressions that the children love. They

love her too, one sits on her lap, another lounges against her shoulder. The evening ends with coloring and pasting and more conversation. The children call to Sister Barbara to come see what they've done, she walks around, giving encouragement and attention. It has not been dramatic or traumatic, but it is important. It is one place where these children don't feel different. Being with each other, comparing notes, talking about their experiences gives them a support they don't get anywhere else.

Each of these children is living with cancer. Some are suffering with disease in their own body, others are suffering watching their brother or sister struggle with disease. For all of them, cancer has re-shaped their lives.

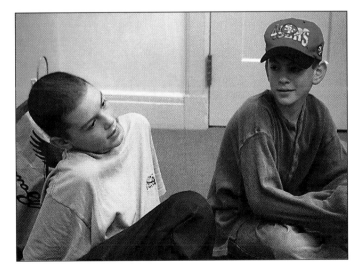

*"Remember, you belong to the people;
     consider them first.
Do not be afraid for your treasury:
Give rather too much than too little.
Filling but a portion of their wants
     would leave the poor in misery still.
Give them what they actually need —
     whatever their needs may be —
Though you may have to give them all."*

Father John Prendergast

Hospitality of the Heart

Acting out of unending love, Lizzie Armer's first mission was visiting people in their homes to bring them physical and spiritual comfort. Every day, the pastor gave her a list of people to visit, then as she moved through the neighborhoods, she would learn about other people who also were in need. She brought food, clean bedding and clothing. She often helped with chores at their homes, and sat with them through terrible nights of sickness. Only by first providing for their physical needs did she feel they would be able to accept the spiritual gift of faith she also brought.

Known under a myriad of names: Relief Work... Social Concerns...Outreach Ministry, the Sisters have always provided for the total needs of their people. These Sisters in Fresno deliver mattresses and clothing to the delight of the families.

Gifts of food include both necessities, like this bag of rice Sister Brenda Marie O'Connor brought to a family in North Kona, Hawaii; and also treats, like the cookies these Sisters always carried with them on their visits around Los Angeles.

Hospitality radiates from their hearts, and makes everyone feel welcome and cared for.

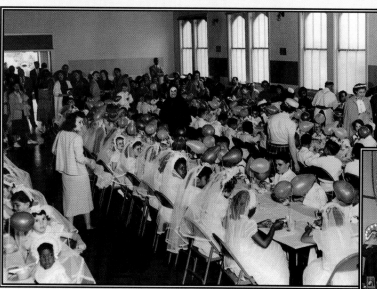

For every occasion, Sisters of the Holy Family provided parties and festivities.

Sewing classes became a trademark of Sisters of the Holy Family, providing young ladies with a skill that was a necessity in 1880, useful by the 1940s, and a rare talent today.

Sister Borromea Russo was still visiting "old people" when she was 90 years old. Mostly she brought them friendship. Everyone looked forward to hearing her cheerful "Hello Dearie" as she arrived.

Sister Brenda Marie O'Connor, campaigning for Bread for the World, typifies many Sisters who have been advocates for anti-hunger or anti-poverty programs.

This deep concern for people's total needs; be they physical, emotional or spiritual, is found in every Sister and Associate of the Holy Family. Their work encompasses an ever broadening scope as they reach out in genuine love to people, and work in larger programs that can impact individual lives.

Broker of Human Kindness

Sister Dolores Molina
Social Concerns Ministry, St. Rose of Lima • Chula Vista, California

Sister Dolores Molina, known to everyone as Mama Dee, sits at her desk in the trailer behind the church, her door is open, and I hear her talking on the phone as I walk up. She waves me in, and continues her conversation arranging for someone to pick up furniture that is being donated by someone else, to take it to a third person's garage who will store it till she finds someone who needs it. When she hangs up she says with delight, "OK that's done, one of our parishioners is donating a whole room full of furniture but I had to get it out of their way so they had space for their new stuff." Another call comes in and she starts speaking in Spanish; someone donated a wheelchair and she wants to get it to a convalescent hospital in Mexico, this man might know how to get it across the border.

While she talks, I look around the office and see boxes and boxes of candy, I ask her about them when she gets off the phone. "It's for the kids at our orphanages. Can you believe it?...I just put a notice in the bulletin that we'd like any leftover Halloween candy, and look at what we got. One gym teacher from Buena Vista Junior High told her girls 'Anyone who doesn't bring candy for Sister Dolores will have to run laps!' So, of course, she got plenty to bring to me. We have enough for everyone at two orphanages. The kids will be thrilled."

This is what she does, all day long; phone calls to solicit, organize and coordinate; and visits to take things where they are needed. Sister Dolores is in charge of the social concerns ministry at St. Rose of Lima. She is a "broker of human kindness", bringing together needs and gifts. Monsignor Duncanson obviously knew the right woman to ask to do this job. It is amazing how many things she keeps going at one time, and with very little paperwork.

Two of their ongoing social ministries are a food pantry and a clothes closet, which are open three days a week at St. Rose of Lima for anyone in Chula Vista who needs emergency assistance. Pat Ziesmer, an Associate of Sisters of the Holy Family, runs the clothes closet and also is a ready assistant whenever Sister Dolores needs help on other projects. This is where people turn for a myriad of needs; and people keep coming as we talk.

A woman stops by to say hi, and mentions she has a Girl Scout troop who could help with a project sometime. Mama Dee says "Could they make place mats? There is a nursing home I know that could use some brightening up, it is a pretty dreary place."

A volunteer from the food pantry comes over, "There's a woman over there who just got a call from her daughter who has been arrested in Bakersfield. The woman needs to go pick up her daughter's baby and bring him back here. She doesn't have anything for a baby, and no money. What can we do for her?" They find diapers, baby clothes and give her a voucher for gasoline at a local station.

The projects closest to her heart are anything that helps children. "I have always loved children, any age, sick or well, any color, all children. A child is so magical." With the Mexican border only nine miles away, she has adopted four orphanages in Mexico. As Sister Dolores talks about "her kids" she pulls pictures out of a shoe box, telling me a story about each one:

"Aren't these the cutest kids you ever saw? According to the Mexican legal system, these children are 'non-persons', because they are children of prostitutes in Tijuana. They can't be registered because they don't have fathers, and they can't go to school because they aren't registered. We started a little school for them, got them desks, paper, pencils, whatever they needed. It looks pretty good in these pictures, it really isn't so nice, but they are getting a little schooling. They are so cute, but I don't know what is going to happen to them."

"This is the doctor's office we set up in 'Zona Norté' (the prostitutes' neighborhood) so the kids can be taken care of. We collect medicine from doctors in the United States, and give it to the doctor down there who dispenses it free to whoever needs it. No one has to fill out a bunch of papers, or sign anything."

"Oh, this is Mama Nana with some of the abandoned children she takes in. When we learned about her, they were all living in one room, we helped her get a two room apartment, and got her a stove and refrigerator and washing machine."

"Here's a party we had for a neighborhood of children last year. We had assembled food to take down, but the night before I went to a reception for a man being ordained as a deacon, and when I walked in and saw all the food, I thought 'Gee I could use some of this tomorrow.' So I went up to the lady who was doing the food and asked her what she was going to do with the leftovers. She said, 'If you'd like it Sister, you can have it.' Then I went around the party and told my friends not to eat. It was great. They packed everything up for us—little sandwiches, cookies. They even gave us the plates and napkins."

She tells me about each place and event, never stopping for breath, the stories keep coming: the orphanage with 150 babies for whom they provide food once a week; the Sisters of Magdala who they help, so they can care for handicapped children, the Christmas gifts that are collected from Assumption Parish in San Leandro [in northern California] and distributed in Mexico, the public grade school in Chula Vista where they teach catechism class after school for children who can't get to the church for classes.

Photos this page contributed. Photographer unknown.

I think she could go on telling me stories forever. Hundreds, thousands of children must be touched by her efforts. She is quick to point out that it is an effort of many people, not just her. This past year she had about 80 volunteers from the parish, and countless others made donations. "People are real good about giving. I've found all I have to do is put a request in the bulletin for what I need, and it comes."

Three years ago Sister Dolores had a stroke and was paralyzed. She was in a wheelchair, had no use of one hand. For six months she couldn't do much at all. It was a time of soul searching for her, and she remembers saying "God, there is so much work to be done. Come on, let me walk so I can go back and help my children." Her doctor said she recovered partly because of her determination. She says she recovered because of the prayers of the children and the many people who love and need her.

Whatever They Need

Sister Sandra Ann Silva
Director of Hispanic Ministries, St John of the Cross • Lemon Grove, California

On a beautiful autumn day, as Sister Sandra Ann Silva and I drive along Highway 94 outside San Diego, she tells me about the family we are going to visit. Victoria, the mother, "is a woman of great strength, whose determination has kept the family whole through years of trials and disappointments...the father, Justino, came to the United States alone, seven years ago to find work, then brought his family here in two groups when he knew he could support them...the two oldest children both graduated from high school with honors." She speaks with great warmth about each member of the family. They are one of scores of families in her parish that are undocumented residents. Like most Mexicans they view the Church as a haven and came there soon after arriving in the United States.

"Contrary to the popular belief of many Americans, Mexicans do not come here to take advantage of us, or our system, they come to find work and provide for their family. Their life in Mexico is without hope, leaving is a question of survival. There are no jobs in rural Michoacan, Mexico where this family lived, government policy destroyed the agricultural jobs, and they had only two choices: go to the United States, or grow marijuana for the American drug trade." Sister Sandra Ann's soft voice blends compassion with authority, and she speaks with a wealth of information about a subject that is close to her heart.

At St. John of the Cross, she is a minister to the Hispanics, which are about half of the 3000 families in the parish. She explains that it is almost like two parishes because they provide all the same services in Spanish as are provided in English. "It is imperative to provide religious services in a person's native language because faith comes from the

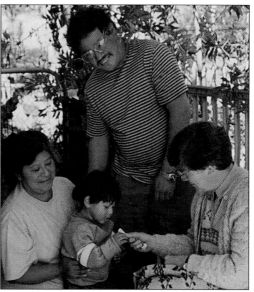

heart, not the brain." She oversees adult education and all the social services and events that are specifically for Hispanic members.

Taking care of the whole person, not just the religious person.

But far beyond that, she defines her ministry as doing whatever she can to help the people she serves, "taking care of the whole person, not just the religious person." That includes being an advocate for them, and I get a quick lesson in Mexican-American relations, history, politics and cultures as we drive. She is very knowledgeable and believes the United States needs to recognize that many of the social and economic problems in Mexico and the rest of Latin America are, to a large extent, our fault. They are the result of policies made to please American interests. Sister Sandra Ann grew up in the San Joaquin Valley of California, but she lived and worked in Mexico for several years, and her friends say she is "American born, of Azorean-Portuguese descent, and Mexican at heart."

We turn into a dirt driveway leading to a plain duplex. The Arreola family knows we are coming, and two darling children, Yvonne and Jonathon, are waiting by the front door for us. They eagerly greet Sister Sandra with hugs, and welcome me with quiet reserve. Everyone is speaking Spanish. Araceli, the 19 year old daughter, becomes my interpreter. They want to tell me how important Sister Sandra Ann has been to them. She is "a friend...a savior...a resource...a support." When they first arrived the Church found them furniture for their bare rooms. When Victoria was sick and Justino lost his job, Sister made sure they had food. Victoria says "when I just need someone to talk to, daily problems or big problems, Sister Sandra is there." Recently she accompanied them at their court appearance to become legal residents.

This family is doing everything right...yet the system is against them ...they deserve so much more, but they never complain.

They applied for their papers several years ago, but the process is very complicated and somewhat mysterious, with seemingly conflicting rules. One of the requirements to become "legal" is to have a reference from an employer which, of course, is difficult because they can not be legally employed. Sister Sandra Ann says, "At the hearing we were treated so poorly—like scum of the earth, and no one bothered to explain anything. The most tense part was when they questioned one of the boys and asked him how and when he arrived. He answered honestly, 'My father came and got us, we hiked over the mountains and through the countryside for several hours...in 1989.' The parents and I gulped because we knew that their application said Justino had been in the United States since 1987, which was when he first arrived. However, according to the court's logic, going back to Mexico for any time, even a day or an hour, negated his arrival date. We were afraid they would tell us the application process had to begin again." With some shuffling and talking, they managed to proceed. Now they have been told, "you have done everything, the only thing left is to wait." Papers could come in a few months, could be a few years. No one knows.

Meanwhile Araceli, having graduated from high school with honors, cannot attend college. No school in the United States will accept her because she is not a legal resident, and she can not go to a school in Mexico, because leaving our country would cancel her application for residency. With money they have been saving, Araceli and her brother recently bought a computer, and are teaching themselves how to use it. The family showed it to us with great pride, and Araceli said when the owners of the Chinese restaurant, where she works, found out she had computer skills, they asked for her help with the bookkeeping. Sister Sandra Ann, always looking out for her people replied, "Great, tell them 'a dollar more an hour.'"

This family is doing everything right, they are loving parents, hard workers, they are like the people that founded this country, and exactly the kind of people I'd like as neighbors, yet the system is against them, and calls them illegal. I see why Sister Sandra Ann has brought me here; to understand her ministry, I need to know her people. She is a gleaner, and I am the grain she has just gathered.

A Very Large Family

Sister John Marie Samaha
Pastoral Associate, St. Joseph Parish • Mission San Jose, California

One after another, women knock on the door of a beautiful suburban home. The door is opened and they are greeted with a bright smile and a warm hug from Sister John Marie Samaha. These 30 women congregate weekly at someone's home for Bible study led by Sister John Marie. It is just one of the many prayer services, Bible Studies and memorial services that she will conduct this week. But this is not where I expected to be when we planned to spend a morning together. I knew she served the poor, the sick, the bereaved. These women are none of those. Sister John Marie told me, "It is not just the poor that need the grace of God. Everyone has different needs. Being with these women is just another side of my ministry." It is also the generosity of these women, and so many other parishioners, that supports her many outreach programs.

Sister John Marie moves at a fast pace, zipping about town in her little car, she seems to be everywhere around Fremont; but when she is with someone, the pace suddenly slows and she is there just for them. Everyone knows her from the mayor to the nurses at the hospital. Tomorrow she will be at Sunrise Village serving lunch to the homeless, then to the nursing home, and probably visiting individuals at home. She is never really sure what tomorrow will hold, "...what I think is going to happen is often changed by immediate needs of people. I just go with the flow."

As a Pastoral Associate, she sees her role as a shepherd, taking care of others. At St. Joseph, Sister John Marie has enlisted the help of 150 volunteers, within whom she has instilled the belief, "With the privilege of being Christian comes the responsibility to live out the message of the gospel." One group has adopted the frail and sick, regularly visiting them at home or in the hospital. Another group cooks, serves and does repairs at the homeless shelter. All of her volunteers are trained to be observant, to look for clues that someone may need help.

"It is better if we can anticipate their needs and volunteer assistance, without people asking. Many people are shy about asking, particularly if needing help is new to them."

One of the group's best known efforts is "Sister John Marie's Pantry" to which people turn for a multitude of services: home repairs for the elderly, paying an electric bill for a family whose father is out of work, help with nursing care for an invalid. Sister John Marie personally reviews all requests for financial aid and, as compassionate as she is, she is also a very good judge of people and is not easily taken in. "She knows when someone is giving her a line," according to Mary Hernandez, an organizer of an annual benefit for the Pantry. "She's not bureaucratic...she'll make the decision from the heart." That's one reason people are so generous with their time and money.

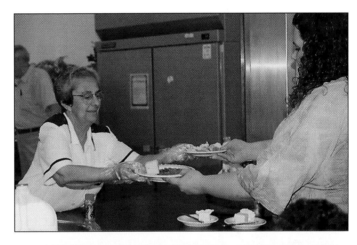

Last year the Pantry gave out $10,000 in food vouchers, allowing people to shop for their own food, and volunteers took dozens of families shopping to buy clothes for their children. This very personal caring is a reflection of Sister John Marie's view of the Church as a family. So she continues about town, taking care of her very large family.

She is with them when they are sick, holding their hand when they are worried, comforting them when a loved one has died, doing what she can to make their lives better. "I'm not under the illusion that I can solve their problems," Sister John Marie explains, "but people need someone to put an arm around them and walk with them through their trouble. That's what I do, and what I train our lay people to do."

Top: *Serving dinner at Sunrise Village, a homeless shelter where all the meals are provided by volunteers from churches and organizations throughout Fremont.* Bottom: *Visiting Margaret Shaughnessy who, although recently widowed and confined by a stroke to a wheelchair, continues to live at home with the help of an attendant.*

Ministry of Friendship

Sister Ruth Faisca
Parish Ministry • Northern California

"Whenever you talk about Sister Ruth, you have to have a smile. Before I met her, I thought being a nun was so serious, but she is so happy and fun...She has been my teacher ever since I came to the United States...I'll always remember that she taught me, God is RUAH, which means 'breath of life' in Hebrew. That is the message she lives out." Max Torres has taken a few minutes away from his kitchen to talk to me about Sister Ruth Faisca. He is the administrator of the Padua Dining Room at St. Anthony's in Menlo Park, where they serve 600 midday meals five days a week, free to anyone who walks in. This dining room is just part of the ambitious social ministry program at St. Anthony's, much of it nourished under the care of Sister Ruth when she was the Pastoral Associate here; and typical of the work Sisters of the Holy Family inaugurate in all their parishes.

I have known Sister Ruth for a few months, and every time I see her, I am overwhelmed with the same joy of her spirit that Max described. She told me with excitement, "I want to take you to St. Anthony's, that is my spiritual home, and I am always pulled back there. That's where you'll get a sense of who we are." Even though she has not been on staff at their parish for several years, Sister Ruth still goes back to St. Anthony's to volunteer as often as she can, and they still consider her part of their family, so today when we arrive, everyone is excited to see her. After a few hugs, Sister Ruth immediately begins to help; packing groceries for a family to take home, bringing coffee

Patty Cancilla, manager of the Clothing Center shows Sister Ruth the surplus pea jackets she bought for a mere two dollars apiece. She has been working on getting these for several months and is delighted 100 men will now have them before Winter arrives.

*You have to love people
in order to serve them.*

to a volunteer who needs relief, straightening shirts on the hangers in the Clothing Distribution Center.

It is men's day at the Clothing Distribution Center, a trailer at the back of the church parking lot where clean clothing, blankets, and sleeping bags are provided free to anyone who needs them. The clothes are arranged on racks and tables, and each man is allowed to select five items. One of the volunteers explains, "We bring in only ten people at a time because we want each person to take his time and shop for what he really wants or needs most." Ruth elaborates, "It isn't enough to just give something to people, you have to be conscious of their feelings, to treat them with respect. You have to love them, in order to serve them."

Loving people, bringing them together, sharing good times, being involved in their lives, forming relationships is how Sister Ruth lives her ministry. "She has been the spiritual guide and counselor for my whole family," Patty Cancilla says. "All five of my kids have come to her at various times for guidance. I'll always remember how she was there for me when my father-in-law died. She massaged my feet, and comforted me. She treats everyone she meets as a sacrament."

Sister Ruth not only loves people, she believes in them and pulls out the best in them. When we leave St. Anthony's she takes me to visit Ann and Mary, two retired women she has been visiting for years. Ann was Jewish, and Sister Ruth was her sponsor when she was baptized a Catholic eight years ago. They all talk at once, laughing and reminiscing. As we get ready to leave, they show Sister Ruth a small statue of the Virgin Mary they want blessed. Ruth tells them "It is already blessed, by you. You have the power of Christ in you."

Rippling laughter and a ready smile, Sister Ruth's trademarks, are shared with Ann and Mary during an afternoon visit.

"I don't want people to put me above them. Being a Sister doesn't mean I am any less human...It doesn't mean I am any better than other people. Thirty years ago, we talked about trying to be perfect, now I have come to understand ours is a spirituality of imperfection. We must learn to balance humility and pride." It is this inclusive spirit, together with her abundant joy, that makes Sister Ruth so cherished by all her friends.

Making a Difference

Sister Elaine Marie Sanchez
Congregational President, Sisters of the Holy Family

Sister Elaine Marie Sanchez stands in the middle of a hostile crowd.

The meeting that just ended was more controlled than last month's but there were still hateful and angry comments hurled from the opposition. This was a Fremont Planning Commission meeting to discuss a project of Affordable Housing which Sisters of the Holy Family want built adjacent to their Motherhouse. It has become a divisive issue in the neighborhood and has brought out more NIMBYism (not in my backyard) than they expected. For three years the Sisters, and their partners in the project, Mid-Peninsula Housing Coalition, have been working on getting approval, and the battle is not over yet. The harder the struggle has become, the more determined Sister Elaine is to persevere. Affordable housing has become a central focus in her mission to live out the gospel...to minister to families and children.

In the 1990s, more people are lacking decent shelter than food or adequate clothing. Helping families today must include providing affordable housing.

So now, after the meeting, she is talking personally with some of the opposition. Having let them talk and vent their frustration, she is calmly explaining how important affordable housing is...how this project is good for the city and the neighborhood...how she is committed to seeing it happen, because it is right and just. To their barbed comments about "those kind of people who will ruin our neighborhood," she responds in a quiet but forceful manner, causing a bit of shame to creep across their faces. She is definitely holding her own, one against fourteen. These angry men and women, who half an hour ago were deaf to the speakers at the front of the room, are at least listening to her. She will not change their minds tonight, but she is gaining their respect and, hopefully, sliding a wedge of light into their minds. It is one small step on a long road for a worthy project. Today, in California, there are more people lacking decent shelter than lacking food or adequate clothing. Addressing this problem is a new expression of the same spirit the Sisters have always had in caring for families.

Affordable housing has become a hotly debated issue in many cities and towns. Like many other sites, this project—although well designed, well thought out, and sorely needed—is being opposed by a well entrenched and politically strong opposition. As she has appeared before Fremont's City Council and their Planning Commission, and attended numerous citizen meetings to explain this project, Sister Elaine has come to the forefront as a leader and advocate for working families in Fremont.

Once again, Sister Elaine explains the affordable housing project designed to be built adjacent to the Motherhouse. For three years, in partnership with Mid-Peninsula Housing, Sister Elaine has been working to receive the needed approval from the city of Fremont. The effort has been long and laborious, but Sister Elaine continues to remain optimistic.

Sister Elaine Marie Sanchez is the current president of Sisters of the Holy Family, and just as she is undaunting in her support for affordable housing, she is courageous in her leadership of their Community. She has unending energy, and a burning desire to accomplish things. Her typical day begins before the sun is up, at the health center where she works out, and ends long after nightfall, at a meeting for one of her numerous committees or advocacy groups.

Sister Elaine is on fire with passion for their mission to serve families and children. For her, the campaign for affordable housing in Fremont is an expression of her dedication to fulfill that mission. She believes the Sisters have been called to make a difference, to stand up for justice, to stretch beyond what might be comfortable, to live out the gospel in bold ways.

Community

*What it means
to be a member of a
Religious Congregation in 1997.*

•

What does the future hold?

Warmed, kneaded, shaped
    formless into formed. Draped,
    spun and stilled
    on the carousel of perhaps.
Our substance born of her fidelity
    will solid frozen be in fire.
The endless pirouettes
    make and break visions on the wheel.
The substance of our very selves
    spun strong
    and unadorned.
Together! Formed!
Once motes of unrelated dust.
Now, lives out-poured and yielding
thrust into impassioned family.
Command not the potter!
The hands pressure as they will,
    and we,
    yielding still,
    become a vessel of the dream.

Sister Michaela O'Connor
August 29, 1996

118

On Being a Sister

A Sense of Community

Gone are the defining attire of habits and veils, the strict rules of behavior, the authoritative structure. These, all familiar elements of religious communities for many years, have been replaced with simple, contemporary clothing, personal accountability and responsibility. Large communal living quarters have been remodeled with private rooms, and many women live in small apartments or homes.

In spite of these external changes, there still remains a very definite sense of community. Sister Sharon Flannigan explains, "I live with three other Sisters. There is no decision I make that does not affect them. Beyond that I also carry a sense of responsibility for all the Community, and always consider how what I do affects both our small group, and the larger Community. When I became a Sister of the Holy Family, I joined a group of women with a common purpose and a common goal. We share our lives completely. That's what it means to be part of a Community."

Being part of a Community is like having dozens of sisters, aunts, and grandmothers, all completely interdependent. Finances are shared, work is shared, laughter is shared, dreams are shared. Community living means accepting each other. It frequently means putting someone else's needs ahead of yours. It mostly means sharing.

Almost one hundred Sisters gathered for this photo in front of the Motherhouse during Chapter Days 1995.

Ministry of Prayer

Equally important as all the external ministries is the ministry of prayer that is so powerful in Sisters of the Holy Family. Although their Congregation has never been cloistered, a rich spiritual life has always been part of their covenant. Several Sisters expressed that when they first entered they were attracted to the active ministries, and it was only through time that they came to understand the ministry and the power of prayer.

Of course, to some extent, every Sister ministers through prayer, both private and communal, and also by living a spirit filled life, but for a number of them, it is their full-time ministry.

The ability to truly let go and give authority back to God, to ask for God's guidance and blessing, trusting implicitly in that judgement, is a gift. Making prayer the focus of their lives is a blessing shared by many of the Sisters when they retire from external ministries.

Many friends and people in need turn to the Sisters for help during dark moments in their lives. In the chapel at the Motherhouse, or the Infirmary upstairs, there is always someone praying for others—one more way they live out their mission to care for families and children.

Receiving a Call

"An inexplicable knowledge of where you belong," is how one Sister described what it means to be called by God to a vocation. "You don't even necessarily want to do it, you just know that this is where you belong." Sister Teresa Marie Stiegler remembers fighting the idea for several years, then finally giving in to a power bigger than herself.

Sisters Jo Marie Arredondo and Ancila DeLaO both said they knew from early childhood that they wanted to be a sister. Their struggles were not with themselves, but with their parents, convincing their parents to allow them to leave for a convent. For their families, the thought of a daughter entering a religious order was completely outside their plans for the future. It meant no grandchildren, no support in their old age, a loss of a family member.

Sister Kathryn Morrow was a society editor for a newspaper 50 some years ago when career women were a rarity. She loved her work, was not ready for marriage so she was dating quite a few men. She remembers she was always restless, and questioning. Then one night she awakened and knew she was going to be a sister. Her friends and parents were amazed and sure she would change her mind, but she knew with an absolute certainty that it was the right thing, and within four months Sister Kathryn was living in the Holy Family convent on Hayes Street in San Francisco.

Each woman has a story to tell about being called to her vocation. Some were easy, some involved struggle, but they all felt a calling, it was not a decision that was theirs to make alone.

That is the first step in a process that spans several years before a woman makes her final vows as a Sister of the Holy Family. Like everything else, the formation process has changed in the past few years. Now it is individualized for each person, providing time for personal introspection, and time to get acquainted with the Community, by living and working with them. It includes study and work experience in a number of ministries. The commitment is for life, and the process is designed to allow an individual to fully discern whether this is where she belongs.

New Kinds of Relationships

Thirty-some people stand in a circle in the shadow of the tall redwood trees. In the middle is a man holding in one hand a plume of feathers and, in the other, a smoldering piece of wood. He slowly circles the group, blessing each person in turn, and then they all join in a common prayer, turning to face the four directions of the wind. Andy Galvan is a Native American whose ancestors lived on this land before it was claimed by the Spaniards, and colonized by Anglo-Saxons.

He is at the SHF Motherhouse giving a program on the history and culture of his people for the Associates and Sisters of the Holy Family. Andy is himself an Associate, along with his father and mother, Phil and Sarah Galvan.

When Sarah was a little girl growing up in Oakley, her catechism teachers were all members of Sisters of the Holy Family, and she loved their classes. Twenty-some years later Sarah had married Phil and had three children who also were being taught catechism by Sisters of the Holy Family, now in Brentwood. The Sisters remember Phil was always available to help them by setting up blackboards and moving furniture. As the children grew, their sons, Michael and Andy, started helping the teachers. Soon Sister M. Cyril Sullivan suggested Sarah should become a CCD teacher. Later Michael and Andy were also trained as teachers, and they all remember days when they would each have a class going on at the same time in their Fremont house, bartering for whose class would get the best room. The boys are grown now, Michael is a priest in Moraga, Sarah and Phil both work at the Motherhouse in Mission San Jose. The Associate Program has given Andy, Phil and Sarah a new expression of their relationship with the Sisters, with whom they have always felt a strong connection.

Associates are women and men who want to be affiliated with Sisters of the Holy Family, who have the same values and charism, and who want to share as part of a community. They are not asked to make lifetime commitments as vowed members do, nor do they take vows of chastity, obedience or poverty. This membership is open to people in all walks of life. Associate Shaun Peterson, co-chairperson of the program explains, "People are invited to be Associates by a Sister or another Associate with whom they have a relationship. They are invited because they are already walking the same path. This is just a formalization of a spirit they possess and a public recognition of a commitment to share the charism with people in their own lives."

"In the beginning, we weren't sure how the program would work or what it would mean," says Sister Jacinta Fiebig who, with three women in her South Dakota parish, formed the first group of Associates. "We just knew we wanted to explore a new kind of membership. It has been a wonderful experience, the Associates have brought new life to the Community."

There are now over 40 Associates, an affirmation of how vital the Sisters' charism is in the world. Several of them were women who at one time had been part of the Community, and had left. One of them, Cathy Olivas says, "I was raised by SHF, and since forever I wanted to be a Sister, I finished my time as a postulant and a novice, but when it came time to take my final vows, I couldn't promise 'Forever.' I was so unhappy, but I knew it was not God's will for me at that time. Thirty years later, I was invited to be an Associate. It has been a fulfillment of my life's desire."

There have always been lay people, starting with Mary Tobin, who shared the Sisters' mission and charism. The Associate Program is a recognition of that connection. It is also just one way the Sisters are reaching out to new relationships. Collaboration with social action groups who have similar goals, and with other religious communities, is also giving them new opportunities to impact larger groups.

Associates Jim and Jean Carpeneti renew their covenant surrounded by many of the Associates they have come to cherish in the past two years. When Sister Margaret Hakeem first invited the Carpenetis to become Associates, Jean remembers asking "Why do you want us? What can we offer?" She told me, "You are already doing our work."

Hope is hearing the
melody of the future;
Faith is dancing to it today.

Facing the Future

What does the future hold? It is a question asked by everyone. For religious women, approaching the 21st century, it is a complex question. They are well aware that some people say, as an institution, their days are numbered. It is an indisputable fact that fewer women are electing to join religious orders than in the past. Is this a signal of the end, or just the normal ebbs and swells of change?

Change and renewal are the instruments of the future. They are also the destroyer of the past, which is disturbing. The challenge is to find the right path, one that is true to the past, but appropriate for the future. Within the Community of Holy Family, facing this challenge is an ongoing conversation. When Sister Elaine Marie Sanchez began her second term as Congregational President in June of 1995, she shared these thoughts about the future during the Eucharistic Liturgy:

"It is not a profound thought when I say that we are living in a time of history when the old and familiar no longer fit. The most disconcerting part of that for me has been that the myths and the stories we share about our Community are not enough.

I treasure our history. It inspires me, but I believe we are being called to walk into the terror of new life and all that it will cost us. We are called to begin writing something new about us. It is an opportunity for new myths to emerge. It can't be done by one, a small group or a leadership team, so the words of the contemporary reading we heard this morning are reassuring.

'A partner is someone you work with on a big thing that neither of you can do alone. If you have a partner, it means that you can never give up because your partner is depending on you.' *

Along with this, the words of Deuteronomy take us further. 'The word is very near you; it is in your mouth and in your heart so that you can do it.'

I am more convinced than ever that we have what we need to move into the future. The gifts are present within us, they have always been present, but do we recognize and affirm them?

May we be partners filled with passion for the mission, partners that are flexible, and partners filled with the excitement of the opportunities we have before us."

* Quoted from the story "Partners" in the book *Does God Have a Big Toe?* by Marc Gellman.

124

The Sisters face both specific issues, and large concepts in charting their future. Will they continue in the same ministries, or enter new ones? What is the role they are being called to play in the life of the Church and the people? What changes in structure or lifestyle are appropriate or necessary to remain vital? Some Sisters share their reflections on the future:

Approaching the Future

We have no blueprint for the future because we've never been here before. What we do have is our passion for mission, our care for the earth and our need to companion one another along the way. Together, relying on God's own Spirit in ours, we explore and discover the future, step by step.

Sister Marietta Fahey

Being present to others means being flexible: it means being open to change and to new approaches; it means being open to risk; it means embarking on a pilgrim journey in faith, not knowing where we will land....We are women of the Gospel; we are daughters of Lizzie Armer. May we continue that legacy in a spirit of simplicity and hospitality.

Sister Mary Lange

The Role of the Church

Church is a way to preserve a culture, it is the one place that links everything up. For people from other cultures, in the Church they can remember their place and their country. It is also the pivotal link from the past to the future.

Sister Kathleen Ann Garcia

As society becomes more technical and impersonal, Church is the one place that can be personal. People need and want to talk to someone.

Sister Gladys Guenther

Our Charism

My hope and dream is that all who meet us will recognize our membership in the future society and Church by these two quotes:

"Remember you belong to the people; consider them first." (Father John Prendergast)

"We will be recognized by our simplicity of life and visible presence among the most abandoned. Our mission as Gleaners will be to serve segments of the population who are underserved by Church and social institutions." (Vision Statement of the Congregation, Nov 1993)

Sister Jacinta Fiebig

I see our Charism being continued well into the twenty-first century. There will be more seniors, poor, homeless, and children who need care. Today our Charism is being carried out by many senior Sisters, myself included. My prayer is that God will send more laborers into His harvest. God has taken us thus far for 125 years. We are all doing His work. With more faith, support and respect for our different ministries, He will see that our Charism will continue.

Sister Catherine Rose Iverson

Ministries

The main focus was, is, and will continue to be THE PEOPLE. To sit at the kitchen table and listen to a woman share her pain, her loneliness, her frustration...or to kneel beside a badly injured person, ministering to his physical needs...you bring to each person the Source of all true healing. I used to think this would come from sharing the message of Christ...teaching, if you will. However, over the years I have found that the greatest "sermons" are lived, not spoken.

Sister Marie Ann Brent

Our place is especially with people from other countries and culture, trying to make them feel welcome in their parishes and to become key participants, not only in the Church, but in the country. We need to make them feel welcome.

Sister Andrea Rangel

While times, tasks and individuals may differ, our ministry of caring and service is consistent. For instance, I am beginning a new ministry with a great deal of "future" in it: studying for a license in Canon Law. Upon completion I will be a canon lawyer in the Archdiocesan Marriage Tribunal, in Los Angeles. The work is about more than laws, it is a ministry of working with people to bring healing and new life to both individuals and families. It is a new ministry that so strongly reflects who we are as Sisters of the Holy Family.

Sister Mary Anne Wittman

Renewal of Membership

I would hope to see a new Congregation ...the former, with its imperfections having passed away. A renewed Congregation, rising to heaven...prepared as a bride for her husband...and God dwelling within. He will wipe away every sorrow...and, among us, there shall no more be worry, sadness, loneliness, unkindness, complaining, rebellion, thoughtlessness and pain, for the old order will have passed away.

Sister M. Cabrini Catania

New members will adapt and continue the charism, but the focus will always be families and children. It is the responsibility of our members today to seek new members who share this focus and are open to the future.

Sister Ruth Faisca

Because in this day and age people are not as ready to make the long term commitment which has always been required by Sisters, we need to consider actively seeking temporary vocations.

Sister Gladys Guenther

Future of Religious Orders

The world is hungry for the kind of bonds that happen within Community life...We provide women a group they can share with, a place where dreams can become a reality. There is a fear that the Church is losing something with a decline in sisters, but they are not losing us. We are here and very vital.

Sister Sharon Flannigan

Change

For 28 of my 35 years in community, I ministered in Day Homes and Religious Education. Then I was in Pastoral Care in our Motherhouse Infirmary, which was where I wanted to be, after leaving the Day Homes. Because of circumstances, I was called to minister to the sick and elderly in their homes. At first it was very hard because I wanted to be with our own Sisters. However, one morning I heard Father Prendergast saying, "You belong to the people, consider them first." Now I know I'm where I belong each time I visit a patient and hear, "I'm so glad you came, I have been very lonely."

Sister Charleen O'Brien

The Church changes because society changes. It is appropriate. The changes that have been made have not been helter skelter. They have been based on the epistles. Change is difficult. It is slower than some people want, and too sudden for others. We need to help people accept change.

Sister Joanna Connolly

The older Sisters have gone through incredible changes. They sacrificed a lot to become Sisters, now the structure and core of their lives is questioned and has changed. When I joined in 1964, it was the beginning of the major changes. So really what I thought I was joining did not turn out to be the case. Today sometimes we feel like nothing is happening, that we are spinning wheels, but when we look back, we see how many changes we've made. It is encouragement for our future.

Sister Carol Reichert

Collaboration

Collectively we will be a greater influence for good in the world as modern communication methods draw us closer over the miles, and as we join our resources with those of other communities to continue the ministries which we no longer have the ability to continue alone. My dream is that children and grandchildren of Associates will join others influenced by our Sisters and Associates in answering a call to Community.

Associate Pat Petit

Listening to the Sisters talk about the future, I am struck by the realization that while most of us plan for our lifetimes, we assume at some point our children will take over and be responsible for their lives; the Sisters are also planning for the continuation of their family. However, it is a much larger family, and their plans are for a much longer future. The task is challenging. They see a future that needs their charism. Their challenge is to make sure their mission continues.